The Audition Process

The Audition Process

A Guide for Actors

Bob Funk

HEINEMANN
Portsmouth, NH

Heinemann
A division of Reed Elsevier Inc.
361 Hanover Street
Portsmouth, NH 03801-3912
Offices and agents throughout the world

Library of Congress Cataloging-in-Publication Data

Funk, Bob.
    The audition process : a guide for actors / Bob Funk.
        P. cm.
    Includes bibliographical references.
    ISBN 0-435-08692-8
    1. Acting--Auditions. I. Title.
PN2071.A92F86   1996
792'.028--dc20   95-47201
                                                                       CIP

Editor: Lisa A. Barnett
Production: Melissa L. Inglis
Cover design: Linda Knowles
Interior photos by Cynthia Lybrand

Printed in the United States of America on acid-free paper
99 98 97 96   DA   1 2 3 4 5 6 7 8 9

*To my parents,
Paul and Betty Funk*

Contents

Acknowledgments

The author would like to thank the following for their help with this project: Garvin Phillips, Cynthia Lybrand, Kimberly Wesson, Vicky Abernathy, Lang Reynolds, the University of Alabama at Birmingham Department of Theatre and Dance, the SETC Auditions Committee, and Lisa A. Barnett.

Introduction

When I was in college majoring in speech and theatre arts, I received excellent training that helped prepare me to be an actor, director, and teacher of theatre. I left college with a strong background in theatre history and literature, speech, dramatic structure, acting, directing, and more. But I discovered, when I arrived in New York City following graduation, that I really did not know how to audition. You see, I never really had to audition in high school or college. Oh, I physically had to go through the motions of auditioning for plays, but because the directors knew me from my work in acting classes and in performances, my getting cast was never totally dependent on what transpired at the audition. As a result, like many other young actors, I got to New York having training and talent, but not knowing how to get a job. Now, as a "professional actor," I had to learn the skills needed to get work. Like so many other actors, I learned about the types of auditions from the trade papers and from more experienced professionals. From a kind director, I learned how to write a correct theatre resume. I learned the tricks of auditioning by trial and error. I observed those I auditioned with and, after a period of time, I learned what constituted a good audition. Slowly, over the next few years, I created a stockpile of successful audition pieces and I learned how to conduct myself at auditions.

This experience is not uncommon among young actors. Often actors work extremely hard in universities and professional acting schools to learn how to act. Many become quite proficient at the art of acting, but they are not taught the art of auditioning.

I wrote this book to bridge that gap. I hope that, by using it, many young thespians can gain some knowledge about this very important part of our profession—auditioning. My aim was to spare readers much confusion and heartache when they begin their quest to gain employment as actors. I hope that, unlike me, they will enter the world of professional theatre with the skills and knowledge needed to get cast. Nothing is more important for an actor to understand than the audition process.

Knowing how to audition will not guarantee that you get every job. There are too many factors that affect the outcome of an audition. But with a knowledge of appropriate audition techniques, material, and conduct; of places where you can go to audition; and of types of auditions available, you should improve your chances of doing well and being cast.

This has been and continues to be my quest as a teacher of acting. I want to give my students, while they are still in school, the skills that will enable them to make a career of acting. Being good is not enough; many talented people fail in this profession. To succeed, you must have talent, desire, drive, and willingness to work hard. In addition, it is helpful to make professional contacts and learn the skills that will give you, the actor, an edge over other performers. One of the most important of these skills is mastering the audition process. I hope that, with the use of this book, you will obtain those skills and begin a successful career as a professional actor.

Conduct at an Audition 1

The Application to Audition

T he first person you will probably contact in any
theatre, in most instances, will not be the casting
director. Usually, you will write or call the theatrical organization and you will communicate with a
secretary, director's assistant, or, in the case of many
regional or state organizations, the auditions coordinator.
Treat these people with much respect! If you have any
questions, they can answer them. If you have any problems, they can help you. If you cause problems, they can
really hurt your chances of getting a job.

For twelve years, Dr. D. Ward Haarbauer has been the
auditions coordinator for the Alabama State Southeastern
Theatre Conference auditions. I think he put it best when he
said, "Think about your goal—to get a job. Everything you
do should help contribute to this goal of getting a job."[1]
Every action you perform prior to and during the audition is
being examined by someone. Anyone you come in contact
with can, in some way, affect your chances of getting a job.
So, from your first contact to your last, be very professional
and personable.

Almost all regional theatre organizations have an audition registration form for actors to fill out. You will need to
complete this form and attach a wallet-size, black-and-
white head shot. This form will be sent to the theatrical

organization along with your audition fee. Here it will first be inspected by the secretary, director's assistant, or auditions coordinator. Make sure you have typed out the form correctly, with no grammatical or spelling errors. Remember, as Dr. Haarbauer stated, "They see the form before they see the person. Directors will make a judgment of you by what they see."[2] Always make sure they are seeing you at your best.

If the form is not filled out correctly, or if the fee is not paid in full, the form is usually mailed back to the auditionee. You do not want this to happen to you. First of all, you have now made a poor impression on the person who inspected your form. Second, audition numbers are usually assigned by the order in which complete audition forms are received. Now, with the form being returned, corrected, and then resubmitted you have caused a long delay in receiving your audition number. At any large audition the directors are more attentive earlier in the process when they are fresh. The higher your audition number, the greater the chances that you will audition late in the day and the directors will be tired and less attentive.

As for the black-and-white photo that you must attach to the audition form, make sure it is of high contrast and very clear. Often actors have a passport photo made. If you do so, make sure it is of excellent quality. Glue it tightly to the form to make sure it will not come off. It has two purposes: first, to identify you so the company will know who you are when you come out to audition, and, second, to make a good impression on the casting director. Remember, directors will see the photo and your form before they ever see you and what is seen will form their impression of you.

These forms will be photocopied and distributed to the casting directors. At a large audition like the Southeastern Theatre Conference auditions, as many as ninety copies may be made; therefore it is imperative that the photo you send be very clear. I would advise any young actor to take his or her photo and copy it prior to attaching it to the audition form just to make sure the copy will be clear. If it does not copy well, have another photo made.

The last thing I want to discuss about filling out an audition form is honesty. These forms will ask you to list things like acting experience, technical experience, and special skills. I have seen young actors who have very little experience lie on the forms about performing in plays or list roles from scenes done in an acting class as if they had performed the entire play. They hoped to enhance their audition form and improve their chances for being cast. Do not do this! The theatre world is very small. You would be surprised how many professionals and teachers know one another. I have been at an audition where prior to an actor's entrance, a director announced to the other casting directors that he knew the next actor and that the actor had not performed in the shows listed on the audition form. Needless to say, no one wanted to hire the actor.

Also, if you list people as references, make sure that, first, you have asked for permission to list them, and, second, that they know you are going to an audition and they may get a call from a company checking on your references. Trust me, directors do check references. One day while I was sitting with a colleague in his office, he received a phone call from a company asking about an actor who had listed him as a reference. Sadly, he told the casting director that he did not remember ever knowing this person. He hated to keep someone from getting a job, but at the same time, he had to be honest about not remembering them. If I am to be used as a reference, I want to know the actor's work well and be able to speak about the actor in a positive way. If I cannot speak positively about an actor's work, I will be honest with the person requesting a recommendation. I don't know of any acting teacher or director who does not feel the same way. Therefore, obtain permission to use someone as a reference and be very honest when completing an audition form.

When Does the Audition Begin?

The audition begins when you walk into the door of the theatre or into the office of the agency. From the moment you arrive you are being watched. For this reason come into the audition well dressed and be prepared to act pleasant to everyone you meet. You can never tell who may one day be important to your career, so be nice to everyone. You also never know who may influence a casting director and who may not. Be sure to look everyone in the eye, smile, introduce yourself while giving a friendly handshake and greeting. Being nice will get you jobs! I have friends in this business who are not great actors but who work all the time. If you talk to those who work with them, they will all comment on how wonderful my friends are to have in a company. "He is a great guy!" "She is a beautiful person to be around!" These actors are hired not because of their talent but because they are friendly and dependable people. I will go out of my way to cast a person with less talent who I know will be punctual, give 100 percent of his or her ability to the show, and be fun to work with, rather than hire a talented person who will not be an ensemble player. What Stanislavski said will usually hold true, "Very talented actors should be sacrificed if they could not contribute to the harmonious atmosphere of the group."[3] Usually, I can tell if an actor is an ensemble player by how he or she acts at this first meeting. It is imperative that you make a positive, friendly first impression with everyone you meet at an audition.

Often at the large auditions, or "cattle calls," actors are brought into an auditorium or audition room in large groups. At the Southeastern Theatre Conference auditions, for example, you are told to wait in a warm-up area. Here you can prepare, vocalize, stretch, or just relax as you wait to audition. A stage manager will come and call out numbers. When your number is called you get into a line. When a group of twenty-five is assembled, your group will be led to the performance space. Usually groups sit in order and wait for their turn to audition. Quite often, this all takes place in full view of the companies who are there doing the hiring. They watch you march in, sit, and they can see you even while auditions are taking place. It is extremely important that you remain on your best behavior during this time. Be courteous to your stage manager and listen carefully to all instructions. As you enter the space, walk in with confidence and always smile. Don't be afraid to make eye contact. While you wait, sit up straight and watch those that audition before you. You do this not only to show support of other actors but to learn from them. By watching others audition, you can check out sound quality and see what areas of the stage are best lighted. A good actor is always aware of the technical needs of any given space. As William Hardy, long-time director of the outdoor drama, *Unto These Hills*, said, "Never hire an actor who walks out of the light."[4] Through observation, you can adapt your audition to fit the space in terms of sound and visibility.

You shouldn't be vocal in your support of others or applaud their performance, but with an amicable look of the eye and a smile you show other actors that you wish them the best. Never think of them as competition, but as fellow thespians whom you hope to work with, not against. Company casting directors can see this, and it can favorably influence them when they watch your audition.

No matter what happens in the audition, always smile and be pleasant. Never forget, the audition begins the moment you arrive and it doesn't end until after you are gone.

How to Dress

David Weiss, who has worked for many years in professional and university theatre, recently told me in an interview, "You know how important it is to wear a costume in a play. Then why is it not just as important to wear a costume for an audition?"[5] David obviously is not saying that for every audition you need to design a costume. What he is saying is that what you wear should be appropriate for the occasion, for the actor, and for the character. We have already seen that the audition begins when you first arrive and continues until you leave. It is important that you dress to impress. This does not mean that you wear trendy clothing. Jeans with holes in them may be fashionable, but they are not appropriate at an audition. I don't say this because I am old, conservative, or lacking a sense of modern fashion or music. I say this because it is true. Remember, your prime objective at an audition is to get a job. When a casting director hires you for a full-time or summer job, he or she is not just putting together a talented group of artists that are needed for a performance ensemble. The casting director is also taking into consideration who will best fit into his or her community and be loved by the theatre's patrons. Where do these patrons come from? Usually from middle-class or upper middle-class families. Who are the people most likely to be accepted into their communities? The answer is clean-cut, all-American-looking actors. It doesn't matter what race, color, or creed you may be; what is important to the patrons is that you be clean, well groomed, and friendly.

I did not understand this as a young man going to college in the mountains of North Carolina. I was a hippie and it was the early 70s. Not long after leaving home for school, I was sporting a set of sideburns that would have made General Burnside envious. I also had a huge Afro haircut that would rival Jimi Hendrix's (a great rock guitarist for those who may not remember). People never saw me wearing anything but jeans and a t-shirt. I was groovy! But all that had to change the moment I decided to audition for a professional theatre. The hair was cut, the sideburns were gone, and the young Bob Funk invested in some more conservative clothes, especially a suit and tie. It is a must! If you want to work, you really need to look clean-cut. So if you are a young woman with a pierced nose, partially shaved head, and hip-hop clothes or a young man trying to look like guitarists Slash or Lenny Kravitz, when you become serious and decide to go to auditions as a professional actor, trade in your look for something more conservative that will help you obtain work.

You should take four things into consideration when choosing clothes to wear at an audition. First, can you move in the outfit? Second, does the outfit complement your body? Third, are the clothes comfortable? Fourth, does the outfit resemble the character? I once had a student who was an excellent actress. She asked for my help in preparing for the Southeastern Theatre Conference state screening auditions. These are auditions held for college students in the region. Each state in the region is allotted so many slots for the Southeastern Theatre Conference professional auditions. Auditions are held each fall to fill the number of slots given to the state at the conference the following March. My student worked hard on her audition piece and I felt she had an excellent chance of winning a slot to go on to the professional auditions. The one thing she did not bring for me to see was the outfit she had chosen to audition in. I was shocked the day of the audition when my student entered the room wearing one extremely tight miniskirt (allowing nothing to the imagination) and a pair of extremely high spike-heel shoes. She had wanted to show off her figure, which she did, but she had forgotten that she had to cross the stage several times in her audition piece. When the time came for her to audition, she could not move as the character would have because of the tight clothing and high-heeled shoes. To make matters worse, she had not practiced the piece in her new shoes and did not walk in them very well. Needless to say, when she slipped and fell, she did not make the best impression on the adjudicators and she was not selected to go on to the professional audition. When I talked with her later she told me she wanted to look good and since she was just over five feet tall, she had wanted to wear heels to look taller. My response to her was that we must accept how we look and not let it get in our way when we audition. If I choose a piece that is appropriate for my age and character type and I dress in clothes that are comfortable, that complement my body, that I can move in with ease, and that are appropriate for the role, I will make a good impression.

Once your outfit is chosen, make sure you wear it prior to the audition. Practice your blocking and make sure it can be done easily in the clothing you have chosen. Ask someone to watch you or work in front of a mirror to check whether the outfit moves well as you go through your blocking movements. The color of the outfit is up to the individual, but make sure your clothes don't upstage you. What I mean by this is that you want to wear an outfit that goes well with your complexion. At an audition, especially one for film, you want to wear things that pull focus to your face, and even more important, something that will pull focus to your eyes. I advise young actors to talk with a costumer or a fashion consultant to discover what colors are best for them to wear.

It is also important to take into consideration the space in which you will be performing. I personally love to wear black because it complements my face and hair. But if I were to audition in a black-box theatre, surrounded with black curtains, my body would disappear into the background and that would not help my audition. If you know your space, then dress in an outfit that will help you be seen in that particular space. For this reason, I always carry extra outfits with me to an audition to make sure that I have several choices of clothes to wear.

You also want your clothes to be comfortable. There is nothing worse than spending a long day in an outfit or pair of shoes that do not fit correctly. At many large auditions, an actor may audition in the morning, then hopefully return for call backs or interviews that evening. To help those in charge identify you, wear the same outfit for the audition and call backs. This may not be fun if your outfit is not comfortable. You certainly will not be able to give the director your best performance.

Finally, we must select an outfit that in some way is appropriate for the character. That does not mean that if an actress is playing a woman in the 1860s she should come to the audition with a hoop skirt on. But for that character she might decide to wear a long, ankle-length skirt with some fullness to it. This will help suggest a period without truly wearing a period costume. Once again, talk with a costumer or fashion consultant for help in finding the right outfit for your character.

To sum this all up, remember to wear clothing that you can move in easily, that complements your body type, that is comfortable, and that in some way resembles the clothes your character might wear.

Your Resume

In business today, people often depend on calling cards to help clients or prospective employers remember them. In theatre it is not a calling card that one is remembered by, but a resume and head shot.

At many auditions, directors will receive your resume before they meet you. From it opinions are formed about you as a person and as a performer. Like the application to audition discussed earlier, your resume will say a lot about the type of person you are.

At a recent theatre convention, I joined a group of directors who were having a discussion about a resume one of the directors had received earlier that day. The directors laughed as they passed the resume around and with a red pen corrected numerous grammatical and spelling errors. "Can you imagine," said one, "how anyone would possibly expect a director to hire this person?" Another laughed and said, "I know this student's professor and I can't wait to show it to her and ask what kind of training is she giving her students." I felt sorry for the young actor. His resume would become an embarrassment to him and his professor.

Make sure this never happens to you. Put time and money into your resume to make sure the paper, print, and content help you obtain a job. Directors for professional theatres receive hundreds of resumes. They look at them, then either contact the actor, file the resume for later inspection, or throw it away. Make sure your resume is of such fine quality that it will draw positive attention to you. So what should the resume look like?

A business resume can be several pages long. Its format gives the reader a clear understanding of the experience and skills of the person. Often I have seen young college actors who use business resumes rather than theatre resumes. A theatre resume is one page long and fits on the back side of your eight-by-ten head shot. The resume is attached to the head shot in one of three ways. First, it can be printed on the photo itself. This looks fantastic but can be quite expensive. Since resumes should change with each new theatrical experience, this form of resume is quite costly to update. The second way a resume can be attached to the photo is to glue it on. Be very careful in doing this. It must be neat, and achieving this can be time consuming. It also has a tendency to wrinkle, which certainly will give the wrong message to the reader. Probably the fastest and most economical way to attach your resume to your head shot is to staple them together. When you do this, be sure to staple them in all four corners. Make sure the paper is aligned perfectly and that they will not become separated. I have had resumes submitted with only one staple. As these are handled, the picture can be pulled from the resume and lost within the director's stack of resumes. This is certainly not a desirable outcome. Make sure they are stapled securely and that both papers match exactly in size.

What information should be included on your resume? First, the reader should be able to determine who you are, what you look like, and how to contact you. The page should also give an overview of your work in theatre and related experiences. Finally, your resume should provide information on how to contact people who know your work and can give you a reference. On the following page is an example of an acting resume.

At the top of the page, in bold print, the actor's name is listed. The reader should only have to glance at the resume to see the name of the actor. Next, a current address is listed. This must be a number and address at which you can be reached. Some actors who are in college may include both a permanent address and a school address. When including an address other than where you are currently staying, inform the occupants about your audition so that any messages can be quickly relayed to you. Company representatives are usually pressed for time and if it takes too long to contact you they may decide to use someone else. Be sure to make it clear on your resume where you can be reached.

Also included at the top of the resume is your age. This may be done by listing either your date of birth or your age. You should never use an age range (sixteen to forty). In most professional theatres and in just about all film projects, directors will hire someone the age of the character. A director in New York once told me that he was insulted by actors listing their age range. Remember that your head shot will be attached to your resume. Directors will look at this photo and the roles you have done and make their own decisions as to what ranges you could play.

From past experience, I have discovered that by listing a specific age as opposed to listing a date of birth, you are usually not considered for an older role, even if you do look older in the

SAM SISKO

ADDRESS: 1861 Jenny Street, Apt. H   DATE OF BIRTH: 6/26/73
Columbia, TN 61234   HEIGHT: 5' 10" WEIGHT: 200 lb.
(726) 928-5467 (H)   HAIR/EYE COLOR: Brown/Hazel
(726) 334-1865 (W)   VOICE: Baritone

REPRESENTATIVE EXPERIENCE

PROFESSIONAL:

The Misanthrope	Philinte	N.C. Stage Company, Charlotte, NC
The Lost Colony	Wanchese	Manteo, NC
The Comedy of Errors	Angelo	Oklahoma Shakespearean Festival, Durant, OK

UNIVERSITY:

Lysistrata	Kinesias	Western Carolina University
Love for Love	Valentine	Western Carolina University

COMMUNITY THEATRE:

The Importance of Being Earnest	Jack	Footlight Playhouse, Columbia, TN

TRAINING

B.A. Speech and Theatre Arts, Western Carolina University, Cullowhee, NC (1994)

Three years of tap from Fleetfoot Dance Studio, Henderson, NC

Ten years of private voice lessons (various instructors)

RELATED EXPERIENCE/AWARDS

Extensive work in unarmed stage combat, competitive power lifting, Civil War reenacting, experienced equestrian, experienced motorcycle rider, dialects: British, French, and Irish, stage carpenter for ten productions, Best Actor Award at Western Carolina University (1993), Who's Who in American Colleges and Universities (1994)

REFERENCES

Dr. Donald Lee, Department of Speech and Theatre Arts, Western Carolina University, Cullowhee, NC 28723 (919-111-2111)

Ms. Cynthia Mayes, Footlight Playhouse, P.O. Box 27, Columbia, TN 61234 (726-340-1233) photo. This seems to be more true of the film industry. If a twenty-six-year-old is needed, filmmakers find an actor who is that age. Because of this, I use my date of birth instead of listing an age. This requires a little time and math to determine my actual age. Psychologically, this forces the director to look more at my photo and decide if I look like the role rather than putting a great deal of thought into my actual age. Never lie about your age and do not leave it off the resume.

Your correct height and weight should be listed. This is important for a director, especially if you have mailed your resume to the company before they see you. Since they only have a head shot to determine what you look like, the height and weight information provides a better idea of how to cast you.

One summer, I was working at a company that hired an actor because he had listed his weight at three hundred pounds and they wanted a Falstaff type of character. They were shocked when he arrived a hundred pounds thinner than he had stated on his resume. At another company, the director was shocked when an actress came in nearly fifty pounds heavier than what was stated on her resume. Do not lie about your height or weight, and if your weight changes, make sure you update your resume.

Since head shots are done on black-and-white film, it is important to include your hair and eye color as well. In addition to height and weight, this provides the reader of your resume with needed information to help determine what you look like. As with your weight, if your hair color or style changes, be sure to update your resume.

Including your voice type will also help the director in making decisions about casting you prior to seeing you in person. Some actors also include their "vocal range" to be even more specific. If you are uncertain of this information, work with your voice instructor to find out.

The main body of the resume is listed under the heading of Representative Experience. We divide Representative Experience into three columns. In the first column are the titles of the plays you have performed in. In the second column are the characters you portrayed. In the final column are the theatres or producing agencies and, if needed, the city and state where they are located.

Listed here should be acting roles, in order of what directors will consider your most important roles to least important. For example, any major film work or work on or off Broadway should be listed first. This is followed by other professional theatre performances such as regional theatre, tours, dinner theatre, or summer stock. Next, list your university performances. Include only roles where you performed the entire script. You should never list a scene performed for a class project. Community theatre performances would be listed next. This would be followed by any applicable high school work.

You may not have very many credits to list in the beginning; just be honest in what information you provide. The time will come when you will need to delete certain shows from your resume to prevent it from being too lengthy. It is more important for your resume to be neat and easily read than to have every bit of information listed.

Under the Training heading, you should list any degrees earned from high school, college, or graduate school. If you have not yet completed your degree, list the degree, the school, and indicate your "expected date of graduation" (the month and year). You should also include any professional schools you have attended or any major performance workshops completed. An example, included on my resume, is that I attended the Society of American Fight Directors' Summer Workshop in 1988. If you have studied dance, voice, movement, or acting from anyone who may be regionally or nationally recognized, include this as well.

The next major heading is Related Experience/Awards. You never know what may get you a job. Here is where you include any information that may help you be noticed by a director. This information makes an actor different from others of his physical type. A friend of mine in New York once got cast in a movie only because on his resume he included that he could ride a motorcycle. The director needed an actor who could ride a motorcycle and no other actors included this on their resumes. Whatever you put here, make sure your skills really are strong. I also heard of a woman who was hired after she told people she could drive a large truck. After being hired, it was discovered that she could not do it well, and much time and money were wasted. From what I was told, she was fired and informed that they would never use her again. Many skills can go here, just be sure you do them well. If you know stage combat, tumbling, gymnastics, ballroom dancing, juggling, cheerleading, or mime, if you do dialects, play an instrument, ride a horse, lift weights, or just about anything that will let you stand out, include it here in your resume. Also include any special awards you may have won, especially scholarships, stipends, or awards in theatre. This shows the director that others have recognized you in the past for your skills as a performer or for your academic abilities. All will help to sell you to the director as an intelligent, talented, and special person.

Finally, you include on your resume at least two references. These are people who will give you a positive recommendation if contacted by a casting director. Be sure to ask these people if it is all right to include their names on your resume. It also may be helpful to contact them when going to an audition so they can be prepared in case a director contacts them.

Your Picture

As stated earlier, attached to your resume will be an eight-by-ten, black-and-white head shot of you. It may cost you, but be sure your photo is of excellent quality. Remember, this is part of your calling card and it is very important that it make a good impression on the casting director.

The most vital thing about a head shot is that it look exactly like you. If that director calls you to come in to audition for him or her after seeing your resume and photo, you had better look exactly like the photo sent to the director. What this means is that every time you change your appearance, you cut your hair, you wear your hair in a new style, you gain or lose weight, and so on, you must have new pictures made.

It is important that the photo looks like you. It is also important that the photo draws attention to your face, especially your eyes. A good head shot usually comes no lower than your collar bone and goes to the top of your head. You do not want to bring into the photo any other areas of the body, nor do you want to show much background. Make this clear to your photographer.

Over the years I have received as a director numerous photos from actors. Some are extremely well done, but many, for one reason or another, are not good resume photos. Kimberly Wesson is one of my actresses at the University of Alabama at Birmingham. Recently, I had a photographer take a series of shots of Kimberly. These should demonstrate some of the most common mistakes made with actors' head shots.

"THE GRADUATION PHOTO"

This is the most common mistake I see with photos of young actors. Here the actress has been told to lean her head and place her chin on her hand. We often see this type of shot in school yearbooks or graduation photos. Yes, the photo looks like Kimberly, but because her hand is in the picture, attention is drawn away from her face. Do not allow your photographer to place you in this type of pose.

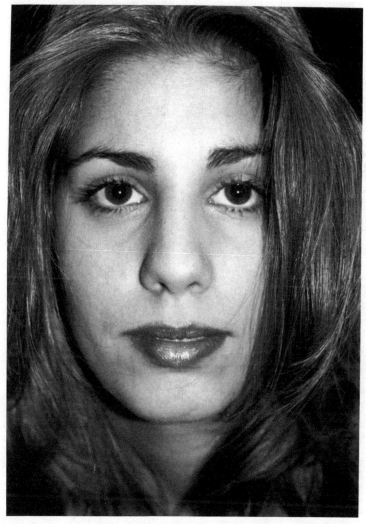

"MY FRIEND HAD A CAMERA AND WANTED TO TAKE MY PICTURE"

You want your photos to be good, so spend the money to have a professional take your picture. In the following example, Kimberly is too close to the camera. We see her face, but look how much of her head is cut out of the picture. As a director, it would not be clear to me just what she looks like. Also, with the camera this close, the photo is not very flattering.

"TOO MUCH MAKEUP"

I have seen actresses who apply stage makeup in preparation for their resume photo. This is very wrong. As you see in the example, Kimberly looks like she should be walking the streets rather than auditioning for a part in a play. Corrective makeup is fine, but be sure not to use too much for this photograph session.

"THE GLAMOUR SHOT"

Kimberly is an attractive young woman who does many modeling jobs. This photo is very glamorous and quite artistic. However, the problem is that with the use of shadows, we do not clearly see all of her face. This photo might look nice as a composite for a modeling job, but for a resume head shot, it is not appropriate.

"I LOVE JEWELRY"

I have seen a number of head shots in which the actor is wearing a large cross, necklace, earrings, or some other piece of jewelry. These pieces may be beautiful, but do not wear them in a head shot. As you see in this example, your attention is pulled from Kimberly's face and eyes to her necklace and earrings. You want the director to remember your face, not your taste in jewelry.

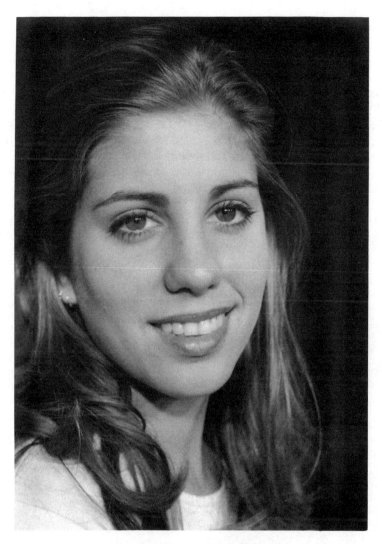

"THE STANDARD HEAD SHOT"

This photo is not fancy, but it is clear and it shows the director exactly what Kimberly looks like. If she gets a call for an audition because of this photo, the director will not be surprised. He or she will have a clear understanding of what Kimberly's face, hair, and especially her eyes look like. There is nothing here to pull your attention away from her face. This is your goal with any resume head shot.

After the actor has selected a photograph for a head shot, there should be two eight-by-ten copies made. One should be kept as a master copy; the second can be used for reproduction purposes.

If the photographer provides reproductions for you, it could prove to be very expensive. However, there are companies who will provide this service at a much lower cost. One such group is Mass Photo Company of Atlanta, Georgia. Using an eight-by-ten, they will print quality duplicates and will also add the actor's name to the bottom of the head shot for identification purposes.

It is important for you to have available at least one hundred copies of your head shot. These photos are needed so you will always be prepared to mail or hand out copies to any theatrical organization for auditions or interviews. Remember, your head shots are your calling cards, so always have them readily available.

Basic Technique at an Audition 2

I served as a state adjudicator for the Southeastern Theatre Conference on several occasions. My job was to watch college students audition at the state level for a chance to attend the Southeastern Theatre Conference auditions in March. SETC gives the adjudicator an audition form to use in order to rate each person auditioning. Four areas are considered: stage presence, movement, communication skills, and acting ability. At any audition, actors are judged in these same four areas.

Stage Presence

When actors walk out onto the stage, they need to, as David Weiss recently told me, "look as if they belong on stage."[6] The actor must be perfectly comfortable in this acting space and radiate an energy that forces the directors to keep their eyes on the actor. Molly Risso, the director of the Oklahoma Shakespearean Festival, puts it this way, "The actor must give the appearance that 'I am important and you need to watch me.'"[7] All of this is having stage presence. Without a strong sense of stage presence, it is impossible for an actor to be successful.

21

Strong stage presence begins with proper preparation. You must know your material so well that there is never any concern about your lines. You must love your material and know in your heart that others will also love it and want to hear it. You must like yourself and the way you look on stage so you are never self-conscious about anyone watching you work. You must be friendly with everyone and never be afraid to look people directly in the eye. You must feel confident that the directors will want to know you and your work. You must speak so that you fill the space with a supported voice and enunciated speech. An actor with stage presence looks confident but never cocky.

As soon as it is your turn to audition, you should walk out to the performance area of the stage, with a sense of assurance and pride, smiling at the audience. If you plan to use a chair in your audition set it at this time. Move in a quick, businesslike manner. Pick up the chair with two hands and be sure never to drag it. Once it is set do not adjust the position of the chair. Now move to your starting position. Come to a full stop, smile, look at the audience, take a deep breath of air, and with a supported voice, enunciate each word as you give your name and audition number. Once this is done, pause briefly as you breathe deeply and then begin your monologue. This pause allows time for your transition from being the actor into being the character. While playing the piece as the character, "take the stage" and make everyone believe you belong there—that this is your domain. All actions are played with pride, confidence, and a sense of fun. Everyone watching you should feel that you are comfortable on that stage. Evidence of this is seen through your body, face, eyes, voice, and movement. At the end of the monologue, stop and breathe deeply, allowing another transition from your character to the actor again. With a smile, again state your name and number with pride and excitement. If you used a chair be sure to strike it at this time. No matter how you feel your presentation went, never allow the audience to see any disappointment from you. Walk off the stage boldly and positively as though you did the piece better than anyone could possibly do it. Maintain this presence until you leave the audition building at the end of the day. All these actions will help you, the actor, to score high in stage presence.

Movement

How we center ourselves and how we move says much about who we are. Body language can often override a verbal message if the two are not in harmony. This will cause your listener to receive a mixed message. It is important for actors to have control of their bodies and to be aware of what their movements, gestures, and posture are saying to others. These actions must be appropriate for the character as well. While entering the stage, keep your body centered and hold your head high. Stand straight and still as you announce your name and number. Once you are in the transition from actor to your character, allow your center to change to fit the character you are playing. If you have done your homework and really know your character's given circumstances, then you will know how this character is different from you in terms of body, voice, and movement. This transition to the character should happen instantly as you go into the monologue.

While playing the character, make sure all movements are justified through the given circumstances and the character's actions in the scene. It is important to have at least two crosses in an audition piece. This will allow the directors to see if you can move as the character. Too much movement, though, is annoying and can take away from the spoken word. Therefore, make sure you are moving because the movement is justified in the text. You should not stand in one spot and talk. Also, if you sit, do not stay in the chair the entire time. Usually at these auditions a chair is provided. You should place it before you do your introduction and be sure to strike it at the conclusion of your name and number. Often, young actors use a chair on stage to represent the other character they are talking to in the scene. This is a bad idea for two reasons. First, if you focus your attention on the chair, the audience will automatically focus their attention on the chair as well, rather than on you. Next, by looking down at a chair, you tilt your head downward. The result is that you hide your facial expressions from your audience; they are forced to look at your forehead rather than your face and eyes. It is better to place the other character downstage of you towards the audience. I always think of the other character as being my height or a little taller. This helps you, as you look at the imaginary character, to keep your face up and open and your body centered rather than leaning forward, which is another bad acting habit. In a play a character may be to your side, forcing you to stand profile on stage. Be sure you never look profile or upstage at an audition. This will cut your face off from the audience and you want them to see your face. Place all imaginary characters you talk to downstage of you. You must keep open to the audience. Actors at times try to make eye contact with the audience. Do not do this at an audition. The directors will be watching you, and if you look into their eyes it may make them feel self-conscious and cause them to look away. Also because they are taking notes, looking at your resume, and so forth, if you focus on what they are doing it may ruin your concentration. If you need to talk to the people in the audience, do so, but look past people, not directly in their eyes.

Some monologues call for the actor to get down on the floor and sit or lie down. Try to avoid these pieces or that form of blocking. This type of blocking makes it hard for the directors to see you. Remember, not all auditions are held in theatres where the audience is elevated above the stage. More often, the audition is in a motel ballroom and the audience is on a flat floor. If ninety or more directors are there to watch the auditions, then those in the back of the space cannot see you if you are on the floor. Nothing could be worse than to audition where at least half of the house cannot see you. I have also discovered that when actors bring their bodies close to the floor, the actor's energy lessens. With only one minute to make an impression, you do not want your energy level to be lowered.

To summarize, your movement is very important at an audition; make sure it is always appropriate for the character and that it is always motivated. Play downstage so that you keep yourself open and so that your face can be seen at all times.

Communication Skills

At many auditions I see actors who move well, who seem believable as their characters, but for one reason or another cannot be understood while they are talking. I have spoken with a number of directors who feel that actors do not put enough work into their vocal development. At an audition, you must make everything you say absolutely clear to your audience. Be sure you have supported breath so that you can project your voice and fill the space. You must clearly enunciate your words so they are crisp and clean. Be sure there is vocal variety in your speech and do not speak in a regional dialect.

I recently had a very talented young woman from England study acting with me. She worked very hard to change her regional dialect and mastered standard American stage speech. As a result, she played a variety of roles while here in the United States and no one ever knew she was from Britain. At an audition, she decided to do a comic piece from an eighteenth-century English play. It was a very funny piece that she decided to perform in a British dialect. At an audition she was told by an adjudicator that she did not speak in a correct British dialect. Shocked, she informed him that she was British and that the dialect was her own. He would not change his opinion and unfortunately she was not allowed to go on to the next level. This adjudicator had studied dialects out of a dialect book, and when my student deviated from what he had learned, he felt she was wrong. This is often the case with dialects. Being from the South, I am often appalled at actors from other regions speaking the southern dialect that they learned from a book. It is nothing like our speech here in Alabama. This is true for many people in any region when listening to someone attempting to do their particular dialect. To be safe at auditions, do not attempt any dialect; just keep the piece in standard American stage speech. This will focus the directors' attention on what you have to say as the character. You may think that you do dialects extremely well and therefore should have no problem doing them at an audition. Whether or not you do a dialect well is not the point I am trying to make. Avoid dialects because they will pull the attention of an adjudicator or casting director from your scene. This kind of audition forces the audience to focus on the manner in which you are doing the dialect rather than listening to what your character is saying. In the short time you are given to perform at a cattle-call audition, this can lead to disaster. Whenever anyone hears a dialect, it is impossible to follow the dialogue for a few moments. For example, Meryl Streep is one of the finest actresses of our time and is a master of dialects. I am in awe of her ability to create such rich, believable characters with perfect accents. Yet in every performance I have seen her do, it takes me a few moments to become accustomed to the dialect she is using. After a short period of time, I understand the dialect being used and totally believe her character.

Ms. Streep will then have another ninety minutes of performance time to entertain me. While at an audition, you will have only a minute or two of total performance time. Even if you are excellent at doing dialects, for those first few moments you will lose your audience. When you have only a few minutes to perform, this brief loss of your audience's belief in your character can lead to disaster. My advice is not to attempt a dialect at a cattle-call audition. Wait until you receive a call back and the director asks you to perform in a dialect; then dazzle him or her with your ability.

Acting Ability

It is not my intention in this text to write a book about acting. There are many volumes about the theory of acting. If in the following pages you do not understand the terms used, I would recommend that you read the following: *The Stanislavski System: The Professional Training of an Actor* by Sonia Moore, *The Stanislavski Technique: Russia* by Mel Gordon, *An Actor Prepares* by Constantin Stanislavski, *Building A Character* by Constantin Stanislavski, *Respect for Acting* by Uta Hagen, *The Technique of Acting* by Stella Adler, and *Acting: The First Six Lessons* by Richard Boleslavsky. These texts have all helped shape my acting technique and should prove helpful to any student of acting.

While at an audition the actor must bring to life for the audience a believable, well-developed character in a very short period of time. As in a play you must make extremely strong choices about who you are and what you want as the character. You must make physical and vocal choices that are right for the character rather than for you. All of this must happen between the time you finish your introduction and begin the piece (the time it takes for one deep breath).

It is therefore important for you to make very strong choices about characterization long before coming to the audition. Unite your character choices to movement and vocal choices so they will be very clear to you and the audience. Once your time to audition arrives, you have a clear understanding of who you are and what you want. In life we play objectives all the time. Not a moment goes by that we do not want something. Our wants guide us in life and on stage. An objective is expressed as an active verb: I want to devour, I want to love, I want to destroy, and so forth. As actors we must identify our character's wants or objectives. By playing the physical actions to achieve this objective, true emotions will be triggered, making the scene believable. Knowing what you want in a scene will guide all other choices. This will inspire all movements and gestures. We never make a movement on stage unless it is justified. In other words, I don't move because I, the actor, feel it would look good here to do so; I move because my character needs to do so to fulfill his objectives.

Knowing your objectives or wants will also allow you to focus and concentrate while at an audition. It is easy to become distracted because you are often playing out to the audience and you are aware of what is going on in the house. By staying focused on achieving an objective, you do not have time to think about what is happening in the audience. This type of focus is much the same as that used by an athlete playing in front of a crowd of fans. At a basketball game, as the athlete dribbles the ball down the court, she focuses on the goal and then makes a shot. The athlete knows the audience is there, but the concentration is solely on making the shot. As a result the audience is ignored. If the crowd pulls her attention for even one moment, the athlete will miss the shot. It is the same with an actor. If the actor is totally focused on obtaining the objective even though he knows the audience is watching, the actor will not be distracted. As a result the actor will not have time to be nervous and the actions performed will appear real to those observing the performance. Thus the actor's work will be believable and that is his goal. For if we are believable to the audience our chances of getting a job at the audition are greatly improved. Make strong character choices and know exactly who the character is. Then you will know the character's objectives and can create strong actions to try to achieve these objectives. All physical actions are justified. Also the voice will be enunciated and projected so all the text is understood. Regardless of the style of the piece all is tied together to make a believable character come to life for the audience.

Twelve Steps to Remember

1. Enter the space with confidence and a smile.
2. Show support for others while waiting for your turn to audition.
3. If singing, politely review your music with the accompanist.
4. If using a piece of furniture, set it quickly in a businesslike manner.

5. Move with confidence to your starting position.
6. Come to a full stop. Look at your audience with a smile, take a deep breath, then give your introduction (name and number).
7. Transition.
8. Perform your piece.
9. Transition.
10. With great exuberance and a smile, come to a full stop, look at your audience, take a deep breath, and repeat your name and number. Strike your chair if you used one.
11. Walk off the stage as if you have given the best performance of your life. If you sang, collect your music and thank the accompanist. Exit back to your chair or to wherever the stage manager directs you.
12. When you leave the space, walk with confidence and a smile.

Selecting the Material 3

Finding a Monologue

Students come to my office all the time asking me to select a good audition piece for them. When I first started teaching, I would hand out monologues to students who would then work on the material and often fail at their audition. It became clear to me that I should not hand out pieces to my students but rather have them select pieces for themselves. The reason for this is that when I give a student material, it is something that I like, be it dramatic or comic. It is something that touches me, something I can relate to. Often, the student will do the piece but never do it as well as I envision it could be done. This is because the piece does not touch them. If you do not relate to a piece, no matter how successful it has been for others, it is the wrong piece for you to do. You must find a comic piece that makes you laugh or a dramatic piece that touches your emotions. Never do a piece because someone else believes it is a good piece for you to do. Do it because you love it and relate to the events that take place in it. Then and only then will you do it well.

Where do you find your material? Do not choose material from popular plays or monologue books. Nothing is more disturbing to an actor than to have someone else do their piece at an audition. It is also frustrating to casting directors to hear the same piece over and over again by a variety of actors. Most actors are lazy and wait until the last minute to look for an audition piece. As a result they immediately turn to monologue books. When a book is written that says, "audition pieces never seen before," as soon as it is published thousands of actors will see the pieces and will soon perform them at auditions. Do not pick pieces from these books for use at auditions. For class work they can be helpful, but not for auditions. The second place lazy actors look for monologues is from popular, often-performed plays. These are usually from a show they had to read for a class, a play they just did, or something they recently saw performed. Quite often, if a play is required reading for your class, other schools are also reading the same plays. Many theatres also want to produce "named plays," shows that are popular and will draw big audiences. You can find lists of seasons for professional and college theatres, and quite often you will see many of the same plays being performed in the same seasons. These are the "hot" shows everyone wants to do. Believe me, at auditions we will often see many of the more popular monologues from these "hot" shows. I'll never forget an audition when three actors out of my group of ten all did the same monologue from Tennessee Williams's *The Glass Menagerie*. When the third actor started the famous "Hogan gang" speech, the directors in the audience actually groaned. You certainly do not want this to happen to you. Another mistake is to pick monologues or songs from the shows currently playing in New York. Many actors love the shows running on Broadway and as a result, pick pieces from them to do at auditions. This is a mistake. By performing pieces from popular Broadway shows you are increasing the chances that you will choose a piece that many other actors will also do.

So, where do we look? I tell students to go to the library and to scan plays looking for large speeches. When you see one, read it. If it does not appeal to you then keep scanning. If it does, stop and see who the character is and put the play aside as a possible choice for an audition piece. This way you can go through many scripts in a short period of time, picking a variety of good monologues. After selecting several pieces, write down the monologues you like. I even keep a scrapbook full of monologues I like so I may use them one day. Don't worry about reading the entire play until the choice of monologues has been made. Be sure to share these pieces with others, especially your acting teacher, to be sure that they are not popular audition pieces and to see if the piece works for them. A piece may be funny or tragic to you, but may not be universal enough to touch others emotionally. Therefore, before working on the piece, test it to see how it will play to an audience.

There are other sources for audition pieces. Don't think that they can come only from plays. I have found many good monologues in novels, short stories, journals, essays, and other forms of literature. One student of mine once created a hilarious monologue out of a religious tract he found in a public bathroom. In it, the author talked about being possessed by a "Disco Demon" and how he could not stop disco dancing. Taken out of context, this proved to be a very funny piece for the actor to do and for the audience to listen to. Another student once created an audition piece out of one of the weekly "scandal" newspapers. In it a person talked about an out-of-body experience and seeing Elvis in heaven. She changed the piece from third person to first and created another very comic monologue.

I love to study history and often read journals written by people who lived in the Civil War era or in the Old West. I have also read journals of people who were involved in the civil rights movement of the 1950s and 1960s. In these journals, common people are writing about facing insurmountable objectives. What they write is exciting, dramatic, and in the first person. It is extremely easy to adapt these pieces into a monologue or even a play. I have written two plays that are adaptations of journals, *Co. Aytch: Memoirs of a Confederate Soldier* and *Women and the War: 1861–1865*. I am currently working on two additional plays, one based on the life of Davy Crockett and the second one based on a journal of a mountain man. The following are examples of three pieces developed from journals. Each is theatrical and builds to a moment of crisis:

First Example:

The nurse said something was wrong with Fisher. Going to his bed and turning down the covering, a small jet of blood spurted up. He had fallen and the sharp edge of the splintered bone had severed an artery. I instantly put my finger on the little orifice and awaited the surgeon. He soon came, took a look, shook his head then walked away. No earthly power could save him. Fisher awoke and asked if he was all right. I had to be the one to tell him he would die. "How long can I live?" "Only as long as I keep my finger upon this artery." After a short silence, he told me to tell his mother that he loved her and that he was sorry. Then he said, "you can let go." But I could not. Not if my own life had trembled in the balance. Hot tears rushed to my eyes and then God spared me the pang of obeying him, for I fainted dead away. When I awoke, he was gone. (Phoebe Yates Pember in *Women and the War: 1861–1865).*[8]

Second Example:

After the battle, I captured me a mule. He was not a fast mule and I soon discovered he was wise in his own conceit (thought he knew as much as I did). You know, they say blood makes speed, well I doubt he had a drop of any kind in him! Me and the mule worried along until I got to a stream, and for the life of me I could not get him to cross. I flailed him on the head, gave a twister to his nose, put a rock in his ear, nothing I could do would work. Finally a caisson came by and the driver said, "I'll help you get your mule across." We tied one end of a rope to the mule and the other end to the caisson and I ordered the driver, "to whip it up!" Needless to say, that mule was no Baptist and the thought of immersion did not please him one bit. But soon the rope proved stronger than the mule's no and we got him to the other side. I got back up on him, he gave a hee-haw and then he took off, first at a walk and then at a run. It was as though he had forgotten something, or remembered something and was now trying to make up for lost time. Anyway with all the pulling and bombasting I could do, I could not get him to stop until we arrived in Corinth, Mississippi! (Sam R. Watkins in *Co. Aytch: Memoirs of a Confederate Soldier*) [9]

Third Example:

I arrived at the pen, a tin bucket in one hand, a milking stool in the other. The cows eyed me with evident distrust and even shook their horns in a menacing manner which quite alarmed me. I marched up to the one which appeared the mildest and set-ting down by her side, seized two of the teats, fully expecting to hear the musical sound of two white streamlets as they fell upon the bottom of the tin bucket. But not a drop could I get! If it is possible for an animal to feel and show contempt, it was revealed in the gaze that cow cast upon me. I had heard that some cows had a bad habit of holding back their milk. Perhaps this was one of them. Removing the stool to the side of another meek-looking animal, I essayed to milk her. But she switched her tail in my face, lifting a menacing horrid hoof. In another moment I was seated flat upon the ground, while my pretty, pretty cow capered wildly among the rest, so agitating them that, thinking discretion the better part of valor, I hastily climbed over the fence and returned to the kitchen. (Fannie Beers in *Women and the War: 1861–1865*)[10]

Wherever you find your material, make sure the piece is appropriate for you. It should be a character who is close to your age. In schools we can cast an eighteen-year-old student as someone who is forty, fifty, or sixty, but in the professional the-atre this will not happen. Pick characters you can play now. Make sure the situation in the scene is universal, so that it will be understood by anyone who watches it. The monologue must also make sense on its own. Often pieces are funny if we know the situation in the play, but cannot stand on their own. An example of this is in Shakespeare's *As You Like It*, act 3, scene 5, when Rosalind talks to Phebe:

> (As, by my faith, I see no more in you / than without candle may go dark to bed)! / Must you be therefore proud and pitiless? / Why, what means this? Why do you look on me? / I see no more in you than in the ordinary / of Nature's sale-work. 'Od's my little life, / I think she means to tangle my eyes too! / No, faith, proud mistress, hope not after it; 'Tis not your inky brows, your black silk hair, / your bugle eyeballs, nor your cheek of cream / that can entame my spirits to your worship.[11]

Like many Shakespearean monologues for women, this one does not really work outside of the play. For it to be really funny we need to know the background and see the interplay between Rosalind, Phebe, and Silvius. If a piece needs to be explained, it will probably not work outside of the play as an audition piece. Also avoid speeches filled with profanity. There was a time in the early 70s when pieces were done to shock the audience. Today most of these pieces will not work at an audition. Remember the types of plays most summer theatres are doing and the kinds of people who will come to see them. Why take the chance of offending someone when it could keep you from getting a job?

All auditions have a time limit. Pick your piece to fit within given time regulations. I always include my introduction as a part of my time as I work on a piece. If, for some reason, the introduction will not be a part of the total time allowed, then I've given myself some extra time. Usually, if the given time is one minute, I pick a piece that reads in fifty seconds. This gives me ten seconds for pauses, transitions, and so on. You will find in most auditions these silences are as important, if not more so, than the spoken word, because it is here that the subtext usually becomes clear. Nothing is worse at an audition than an actor who rushes to get out all the words of his monologue without allowing time for transitions. As I tell my students, it doesn't pay to try to pack a steak into a vienna-sausage length of time! Be sure to time the audition piece so that it will never go over the time allotted for the audition.

All audition pieces need to go somewhere. This means they should build to some crisis. Try to avoid what I call, "The there I was speech." Often you will find monologues that are beautiful. These speeches describe a place, a person, or time. Often they can have the feeling of a beautiful poem, but nothing dramatic happens. For a play to be interesting, it requires conflict. Without some type of emotional build an audition piece will die. At the same time be careful that you don't pick the speech that is the climax of a play. Moments of high emotion are easy to play when the playwright gives you an hour or two of dialogue to build to that point, but it can be hard to reach believably in less than one minute of dialogue. The audition piece must build to some moment of crisis, but it should be believable that you can reach this moment honestly in the time given. If your piece is tragic, make sure, as you play the emotion, that your voice is not strained and that all words are clearly enunciated and articulated. You must maintain vocal control.

Sometimes people will choose pieces from recent plays they have performed. The danger with this is that you will perform it using the same blocking as you did in your production. Remember, it must be changed so that the piece plays out toward the audience. Also make sure that the piece does not require responses from characters not seen on stage. The work must stand alone.

All actors should put together a repertoire of monologues that they can do at a moment's notice. At most regional auditions, you will first present a piece for all the companies to view. After seeing you, the individual companies will decide whether or not they want to give you a call back. The call back is held in some location other than the main audition space. Each participating company will have its own space. Depending on where the audition is held, the size of the space may vary. At a university, it could be a classroom. At a convention center, it may be a motel room. Usually, a call back sheet is posted for each participating company. It will tell you where to report. After looking to see what companies called you back, you will then go to each space listed and sign up for a call back time.

When you report to the call back, a variety of things may happen. They may just want to interview you. They may want you to repeat your audition piece again. They may ask you to do a "cold reading" from the play they are doing. Or they may ask you to perform other monologues or songs. Whatever they ask you to do, you must be prepared. In order to prepare for this call back, it is best to have at least five audition pieces prepared: a modern drama, a modern comedy, a classic tragedy, a classic comedy, and a piece that shows you can play a character different from your type. You should also have prepared two songs and bring with you the required sheet music and if possible a cassette recording of the accompaniment. Let's look at each of these pieces.

The Modern Drama

This piece will be a character you can play now. He or she is your character type and close to your age. The piece will show the character in crisis, allowing the director to see you play honest emotions. The length of this piece should be around one minute. As stated earlier, make sure it is not from a "hot" play. It does not have to be from a play, but must have a beginning, middle, and end reaching some sort of climax.

The Modern Comedy

As stated earlier, the comic piece should be a character you can be cast as now, close to your own age and character type. This piece is also a minute long and should be funny, not only to you, but to the audience as well. At recent auditions I have witnessed young actors telling jokes for a comic piece. Be careful of this. Remember, we want the piece to go somewhere. It has a beginning, middle, and end. It also shows a strong character. Do not just prepare a piece of fluff. Make sure the piece shows a strong, three-dimensional character striving to achieve some objective. Usually, if this is done, the character seems real to your audience and at the same time will be funny.

The Classic Tragedy

In these times, many companies do a variety of plays in a season. Therefore we actors should be prepared to show the casting director that we can handle the classics. Ancient Greek and Elizabethan tragedies, when done well, show that the actor has great control of both voice and body. They also demonstrate that the actor has an understanding of text and use of language and the ability to develop a strong character. To best sell yourself as a versatile performer, it is important to include these works in your repertoire of monologues. These pieces can be a little longer than your modern monologues, but I would work to keep them under two and a half minutes in length. At many auditions actors are told if they do not do Shakespeare well, then do not do Shakespeare at all. I agree. It is extremely hard to do a monologue from a Shakespearean production without being compared to someone else who did the role and, in most cases, someone famous. If you do Shakespeare, avoid doing any of his major characters and plays. *Macbeth, Romeo and Juliet, Hamlet, Julius Caesar, Othello, The Taming of the Shrew, A Midsummer Night's Dream, Richard III,* and *King Lear* are all plays you want to avoid. Directors have seen these plays done many times and know them well. They have preconceived ideas of how speeches should be interpreted and performed. To do it differently may hurt your chances to be hired. If you want to perform Shakespeare, choose his plays that are not often produced and do supporting characters rather than the leads to lessen your chances of being compared to others. Plays I suggest are *Henry VI* (parts 1 and 2), *Coriolanus, Titus Andronicus, Timon of Athens, King John, Cymbeline, Henry VIII,* and *Pericles.* This should help to keep you from being compared to others. Shakespeare also had a number of contemporaries whose plays are not done that often. You will find that these plays contain powerful speeches that show directors that you can create a believable character and that you can handle the language of a period play. You may want to inspect some of their plays. Playwrights I suggest are Christopher Marlowe, John Ford, Cyril Tourneur, John Marston, Thomas Dekker, Ben Jonson, Thomas Middleton, John Webster, Robert Greene, Jean Racine, and Lope Felix de Vega Carpio. You can also consider the Greek playwrights: Aeschylus, Euripides, and Sophocles. These plays have many monologues in them and, because they are not produced that often, they allow you to do a period monologue without being compared to other performers.

The Classic Comedy

There are many comic sources to choose from. Greek, Roman, Elizabethan, French neoclassic, Restoration, and eighteenth-century comedies are all filled with funny speeches and characters. As with the classic tragedy, you want to choose a piece less than two and one half minutes in length. Classic comedies can really allow you to show a director a command of language and use of your body. Here are a few playwrights you may want to explore. Greek and Roman playwrights include Aristophanes, Plautus, and Terence. From the Restoration and eighteenth century you may choose Aphra Behn, Mary Griffith Pix, Susanna Centlivre, Mercy Otis Warren, Frances Burney, Hannah Cowley, William Wycherley, Sir George Etherege, William Congreve, George Farquhar, Henry Fielding, Oliver Goldsmith, and Richard Brinsley Sheridan. You may also want to consider the French playwrights Moliere and Pierre Carlet de Chamblain de Marivaux or the Italian playwright Carlo Goldoni.

The Stretch Piece

This should be a modern piece about one minute in length. It will show your director that your are capable of doing something other than your character type. I always tell my students that this is the character you would love to perform, but probably could never be cast as. For example, I have always wanted to play Don Quixote in *Man of La Mancha*. He has some brilliant speeches, but due to my physical size and lack of singing ability, I would never be cast in that role. Yet in the past I have performed a monologue from the play just because of its power, beauty, and the fact that I could feel everything that is said in the speech. With this piece, have fun performing for your casting director, because you are getting to do something you may never have the chance to do on a professional stage. At the same time you may persuade the director that you are capable of doing roles outside of your physical type. This can open up other job possibilities for you, but only if the piece is done well.

The Cold Reading

Most auditions you will attend outside of the large cattle-call auditions will require you to read from the script being produced. Even at the cattle-call auditions, if you get a call back you will probably be asked to read from the script with another actor or actors. This type of audition is referred to as a cold reading. At this reading you will be expected to make the printed word come to life and as you read, show the director that you can create a strong characterization and play off other actors. How do you do this? If at all possible, try to read the play prior to coming to the audition. It will help you to read it several times. First, read it for enjoyment and to learn the story. Figure out which characters are your character type and, on your second reading, study them closely. These are the characters you will most likely be asked to read at the audition. Know them, know their objectives, know their given circumstances, and be able to make strong decisions about how they move, talk, and relate to all the other characters. This will allow you, at the audition, to make strong character choices as you bring the character to life. You also want to look up any words that you do not know and make sure you know what they mean. As you read the play again, read it out loud and be sure you can pronounce everything. If you are uncertain about any pronunciation, be sure when you go to the audition that you get there early enough to ask the director or one of the assistants how to pronounce the words you have questions about. This shows the director and staff that you have prepared for the audition and that you want to do well. With your last reading of the play look for possible scenes that a director may choose to read at the auditions. Now you can spend extra time on these scenes so that at the audition you will be able to look in the faces of the other actors while reading, rather than keeping your face in the script the whole time. Sharing scenes at auditions is extremely important, so by knowing the scenes very well, you will be free to move and to play off the other actors. Your audition will be more powerful because of this.

Often, theatres are doing new scripts or plays you have not had a chance to read. Be sure to get to the audition early. This will allow you to ask what scenes are going to be read and to get a copy of the script and/or scenes so you can read them, familiarize yourself with the characters, and make strong choices about who they are and what they want in each scene. You can also discover any words you do not understand or can't pronounce and have time to remedy this situation. Prior to the time the audition begins, do not be afraid to ask questions about what will be required. As a director, I'd rather an actor be informed and do a good job than to stay silent and give me a poor audition. At a cold reading, the director is looking for people who work well together and who give the strongest performances.

For this reason, the more familiar you are with the script, the stronger your audition will be. Knowing the script will allow you to make eye contact with the other actors, to actively pursue the character's objectives, and to move freely around the stage as needed. There is nothing worse at an audition than watching actors who stand in one spot and read every word without looking up and sharing the scene with the other actors. With your nose in the script it is impossible to see what other actors are doing. This will also force you to stop listening to your fellow actors. Listening is vital to create communion on stage. As Stanislavski says, "To be in communion with another person on stage means to be aware of that person's presence, to make sure that he hears and understands what you tell him and that you hear and understand what he tells you. An honest unbroken communion between actors holds the spectator's attention and makes them part of what takes place on stage."[12] The result will be an honest and exciting portrayal of a character, and each moment will appear to happen for the first time. Your cold reading will stand out, because it will be believable.

Do not be afraid to take chances with the cold reading. I once heard a director say that at auditions he only remembered the worst and the best. Those in the middle were forgotten. I love to watch an actor try something new. Of course, whatever you choose, it must be correct for the character to do in this situation. You also want to find something exceptional about this person you are playing and bring this quality to life on the stage. This will force the director to take notice of you. If it is the wrong choice, the director will tell you and then you can try something else appropriate for the character. As Uta Hagen says, "We must overcome the notion that we must be regular. It robs you of the chance to be extraordinary and leads you to the mediocre."[13] Let me give you an example of what I mean here. In the movie of *Othello*, Laurence Olivier, as Othello, makes the choice to point at another character with his pinky finger and drive the character to the floor. Any other actor would have done the same action with his index finger or perhaps with his whole hand. But Olivier shows the power of this Othello over the other character by pointing at him with his weakest digit. The result is believable, right for the character, and, because it is extraordinary, it will be remembered by the audience. An ordinary gesture was made extraordinary. Never be afraid to go out on a limb; make choices at auditions that, while correct for the character, are unique, allowing you to be remembered. That is how you get hired over other actors.

The Song

As an actor, the more things you do well the better your chances are to get work. I have often heard other directors refer to an actor as "a triple threat," one who can act, sing, and dance well. These actors really increase their chances of getting work because they can be cast in many types of roles in a wide range of styles of plays. Acting students who attend the mass auditions soon discover that their colleagues who act and sing well seem to get more call backs. I have heard students tell other students, "You better prepare a song and a monologue if you go to the Southeastern Theatre Conference auditions or you will not get any call backs." Hearing this, young actors search frantically for a song they can sing at the audition. Finally they come to me and ask, "What should I sing?" The answer for my students and for you is, if you do not sing well, do not sing at a cattle-call type of audition. The key word here is *well*. If you do not sing well, singing at an audition will only hurt your chances of getting a job. You will better serve yourself by taking the time you put into working on a song into working on your monologue. Directors want to hear strong, trained voices at a singing audition. Anything less is a waste of their time and yours. You may ask, "Who determines if I sing well?" You need to take voice lessons from a professional singing teacher. This teacher will best be able to ascertain if you are good enough to sing at an audition. Private voice lessons will cost you money. But if you are serious about making theatre your career, you must take the classes that will best prepare you to obtain work. As you search for a voice teacher, be sure you find one who has a love and understanding of musical theatre and who will have a knowledge of musical theatre selections.

When you, your director, and your voice teacher feel that you sing well, it is time to look for audition pieces. As with the monologue, you want to find songs that you relate to and enjoy singing. You can't "sell" a song to others if you do not understand it and if it does not move you emotionally. Next, you want to avoid the "hot properties" or popular shows. As with the monologue, stay away from the shows currently playing on Broadway or that are often done in theatres around the country. Directors get tired of hearing the same pieces again and again, so try to find something more obscure. You must be careful in your search to find obscure material. You can do songs that are not from musicals, but make sure they sound as if they are. Unless you are auditioning for a country music theme park, avoid doing country-and-western songs. Unless you are auditioning for a rock opera, avoid rap, hard rock, or rock-and-roll songs. I would also advise students to avoid auditioning with hymns and folk songs unless the show you are auditioning for uses these forms of music. Try to find songs that will reflect the style of songs performed in the musicals you are auditioning for.

Also, like the monologue, the song must say something about you while showing off your best attributes. To sing a pretty song is not enough; you must make the piece come to life! To do so, you must be able to act it. Acting the song will allow you to show the director a different character from the one in the monologue.

The musical selection should build to a climax, both emotionally and technically. You should start comfortably within your vocal range and build to a high note. In sixteen bars of music you should cover the lowest and highest notes that you can sing with confidence. This allows you to show the director the scope of your vocal range.

Choreography is not necessary. In fact, often too much movement with a song will distract from the piece. I have been to auditions and have seen young actors try to copy choreography from a recent show while singing their song. Instead of impressing the director, this added choreography taken out of context of the musical can make the performer look silly. You need only to sing your song with power and conviction to get that needed call back. If you want to show them you can dance, then go to the dance auditions.

Sixteen bars of music is more than enough to show the director that you have a good voice. Within the first few seconds of a song, the director usually knows if you have a good voice or not. If you have a strong singing voice, the director knows you are good already, so why waste the director's time and yours by continuing to sing? If you are a mediocre singer, the longer you sing, the more chances you are giving yourself to make a mistake and thus look bad. If you are a bad singer, the more you sing, the more painful it is for the director to listen to you. If you sing too long you may ruin your audition. Regardless of your skill level, keep your presentation short. It is always better to finish an audition with the director wanting to hear more. This is why they have call backs. If the director needs to hear you sing again, he will have you do so at your call back. Always leave your audience wanting to hear more.

At most auditions you will need to bring in your sheet music and give it to the accompanist just prior to going out on stage to perform. Be polite to this person; you want to do well and he or she can make you look good or bad. The accompanist is instructed to play what is written. He or she will not transpose your music or improvise for you. Make sure that the music you bring is written in your key and that you have rehearsed it prior to the audition with another accompanist. I always instruct my students to give their music to accompanists with whom they have not worked and ask them to play it. This is to make sure the sheet music can be read easily and that it is in the key and tempo you are used to singing in. Accompanists at auditions have only a few seconds to look at your piece; for your own benefit make sure it is easy to read. You will show your accompanists where you will begin and where you will end. Make the cues clear to them so they know exactly when to start and to stop playing. Mark everything clearly in your music because you want to help them do the best job possible playing for you. One thing many actors do not think about is whether or not the piece of sheet music will stand on its own and not fall down while it is being played. If it will not stay up, it may be a good idea to tape the sheet to a stiff piece of cardboard. You should also prepare the sheet music so that the accompanist does not have to worry about turning the pages. If you make this person's job easier, your thoughtfulness will be appreciated and that could help your audition.

Some auditions allow you to bring in a taped accompaniment. If you choose to use a cassette tape, make sure the recording is of the highest quality. A bad tape can be hard to hear or it can distract the director, causing him or her not to listen to your voice. If using a tape, the actor will take it to the accompanist, who will place the tape in the player. At these auditions, the accompanist is usually told to start the tape and to stop it and to do nothing more. The volume is often preset for everyone and does not change. It is vital that your music be cued tightly to your starting point. You do not want to wait for the music to begin while you are on stage; even worse, you do not want it to start somewhere in the middle of your piece. I'll never forget a young man I once taught who had a beautiful singing voice. I encouraged him to use sheet music but he had a friend make a tape for him. His logic was that he would do better using the taped music he had rehearsed rather than depending on an accompanist who might not be able to play his song in the key and tempo he had rehearsed. The actor worked hard on the song and felt that he was ready. On the day of the audition, he remembered his tape, but forgot to cue it to the starting point. When the music began, it was in the middle of the first verse. The actor panicked on stage because he had no idea where the music was until the chorus began. He tried to sing with the tape, but being on the wrong words and notes did not make the best impression on the directors. As a result, a very talented actor received no call backs at the audition. So you are taking a greater risk when using a cassette tape rather than having the music played live. But if you do use a tape, make sure it is cued to the starting place and make sure you explain to the accompanist when you want it to begin and end.

Finally, make sure that the taped music you use has studio-quality sound that will be clear regardless of the quality of tape recorder it is played on. Some large auditions will allow actors to sing a cappella, but this is not done often. It is best to bring your sheet music and sing with an accompanist or to have musical accompaniment on tape.

One of the best actors I have ever had the pleasure to know was my graduate school roommate, Andy Alsup. Andy was a triple threat; he could sing, dance, and act extremely well. Once, for an audition at the Southeastern Theatre Conference, he picked a piece that I feel is a great example of a good audition song. It is "Manchester, England" from the musical *Hair*. This is an excellent song, but it is not one of the "hit" songs from this show. Therefore it is not performed as often as the songs "Aquarius," "Easy to be Hard," "Good Morning, Starshine," "Hair," or "Let the Sun Shine In." This song allowed Andy to show his vocal range in a very short period of time. In less than sixteen bars of music he would thrill directors with his powerful singing voice and leave them wanting more. Because his selection was at the beginning of the song, it was easy for him to show the accompanist where to begin and end. And because he started at the top of the piece the accompanist did not have to turn any pages. Since the introduction to the song was played, Andy could easily find his first note. This song allowed Andy to make a positive impression on his accompanist and on casting directors and as a result, he got work.

As you prepare for future auditions, begin to collect a variety of songs that you sing well. Keep the sheet music in a file that can be taken to any audition. It may also help to have your songs recorded on a cassette tape that you can also take to auditions and call backs. These songs can be used at auditions and call backs to show the director that you can sing a variety of styles of music. Directors will be impressed if they ask if you are prepared to sing something else for them and you can give them several songs to choose from. As with the monologue, having a variety of songs prepared to do at a moment's notice will help you to be more relaxed at auditions and will greatly enhance your chances of getting cast.

Professional, Regional, and State Auditions

4

Auditioning Out of New York or Los Angeles

For actors outside of New York City or Los Angeles, there are many opportunities to audition for professional theatre companies. These companies can be found in many cities around the country. Each holds auditions at various times during the year. As an actor, it is to your advantage to discover what theatres are in your area. Contact them and submit your resume and head shot. Find out when they hold auditions and make a request to have an opportunity to audition. Many states also have state film commissions. These state agencies are usually found at your state capital, and they have information about any future film projects. Be sure to contact them to obtain information on upcoming auditions.

Finally, many states and regions around the country have theatre associations that run professional theatre auditions. Often you have to belong to these organizations and live in the state or region to be allowed to audition. As an actor, find out about your state and/or regional theatre organizations and join them. By belonging to these organizations and attending their conventions, you can not only get information on auditions but also make needed contacts to help you get work.

The following is a listing of some of the main state and regional theatre organizations and information about their auditions.

Illinois Theatre Association

Illinois Theatre Association, Theatre Building, 1225 W. Belmont Avenue, Chicago, IL 60657

Contact person: Wallace Smith, Executive Director

Auditions take place generally around the second week of March and are usually held in Chicago. Those eligible to audition include students in good standing in Illinois colleges and universities, actors new to Illinois and Chicago, and nonprofessional affiliates of an Illinois community theatre. The application to audition deadline is near the end of February. There is an audition fee, nonmembers thirty dollars and ITA members twenty-five dollars.

Audition Format: The nonmusical limit is three minutes and should include two contrasting monologues. The musical limit is four minutes and may include sixteen bars of a song. Musical auditionees must bring sheet music in their own key. An accompanist is provided for the audition. No one is allowed to sing a cappella or to use a cassette tape.

Indiana Theatre Association

Indiana Theatre Association, Butler University Theatre, 4600 Sunset Avenue, Indianapolis, IN 46208-3443

Contact person: Linda Charbonneau

Auditions are held generally around the first week of February. In 1995, they were held in Indianapolis. Around twenty companies are represented at this audition. The application deadline is around the last week of January. To audition, you must be at least eighteen years old. Each applicant to audition must be recommended by a professional or academic director who is acquainted with the student's work. Members of Equity may apply without a recommendation but must list references. The fee is twenty dollars; group rates are available to students whose departments are organizational members.

Audition Format: Each actor is given a total of two minutes to audition, with or without a song. Timing begins after the actor's name and number are given. An accompanist is provided for the audition. Actors cannot sing a cappella or use a tape cassette. The accompanist will not transpose your music and the sheet music should be clearly marked. Sixteen bars of a song are suggested for those that sing.

The Indiana Theatre Association provides those who audition a list of audition tips. Suggestions are made concerning the actor's preparation, selection of material, dress and deportment, and behavior at call backs. Many of the same ideas that have been covered in earlier chapters of this book are stressed in this list of tips. For example, since you are allowed two minutes for your performance, actors have the possibility of performing more than one piece. "When choosing more than one selection, see to it that they offer a strong contrast and sense of variety (comic vs. dramatic; verse vs. prose; odd vs. normal; classical vs. contemporary)." The organization is very strict with the two-minute time limit, which begins "after you have given your name and number." The call backs at this audition are "posted after each hour of auditions and it is the actor's responsibility to sign up for an on-site appointment with the producer."[14] The complete list of audition tips is provided by the organization within their registration packet.

Institute of Outdoor Drama

Institute of Outdoor Drama. CB #3240, Nations Bank Plaza, University of North Carolina, Chapel Hill, NC 27599-3240

Contact person: Cindy Biles, Auditions Coordinator

Auditions are held around the third week of March at Chapel Hill, North Carolina. Approximately fifteen companies are represented at this audition. Anyone who is eighteen years of age and has had previous training and experience in theatre is eligible to audition. Actors must be available for the entire summer season. A statement of support from a teacher or director is required. The application deadline is around the second week of March. There is a fifteen-dollar audition fee that must be submitted with the application to audition.

Audition Format: Acting, singing, and dance auditions are not held at the same time. Actors should prepare a one-minute monologue and singers should prepare a one-minute song. An accompanist is provided for the singer, who may sing a cappella but who cannot use a taped accompaniment. For dance auditions, a choreographer leads a warm-up and combinations using modern, ballet, and folk choreography. The Institute of Outdoor Drama supplies auditionees with excellent guidelines for singers. These guidelines would apply to any audition:

> Please prepare your music for the accompanist; he wants your audition to go smoothly as much as you do.
> 1. Bring a copy of your music that is legible and in your key. The accompanist will not transpose it on the spot. If necessary you may need to pay an arranger to write out the song in your key and style.
> 2. Tape pages together or put them in a notebook so they don't fall off the music holder during your audition! If you are using a music book, be sure it is broken in and the pages won't turn by themselves.
> 3. Be sure your music is clearly marked for any deviation in tempo or text (many accompanists follow the text as well as the music).
>
> At the Audition:
> 1. Tell the accompanist what song you will be performing. If you have any special instructions, be sure to give them to the pianist before you start. Tell the accompanist if you plan to repeat any section of the song. If you plan to take only second endings, please mark through the first ending and instruct the accompanist of your intentions.
> 2. Give your tempo to the accompanist in accurate, professional terms (medium is a vague term).
> 3. Expect the timer to interrupt you when your minute is up; that's his job and it doesn't have a negative impact on the result of your audition.
> 4. After your audition, go to the accompanist to collect your music. Be sure to thank him.[15]

The above "Guidelines for Singers" are included within the Institute of Outdoor Drama's confirmation packet.

Mid-America Theatre Conference

Mid-America Theatre Conference, 12528 South Alcan Circle, Olathe, KS 66062

   Contact person: Glenn Q. Pierce.

   Auditions generally take place between March 10 and 20 each year. The site of the audition changes from year to year. In 1995, it was held in Kansas City, Missouri. About fifty companies are represented at the audition. Over 450 actors audition over a three-day period.

The auditions are combined Equity and non-Equity. The application deadline is about one month prior to the audition date. Late registrations are accepted on a first-come, first-served basis until all audition/interview slots are filled. The fee is thirty dollars and those who register late pay thirty-five dollars.

Audition Format: Each auditionee should prepare a maximum of two minutes of material. The material may include a monologue, or monologues, and/or a song or songs. An accompanist is provided. If you are singing, bring your sheet music and make sure it is easily readable and in the correct key. A cassette tape deck is provided if you want to use a cassette recording. You should be prepared to bring at least twenty-five head shots and resumes to the audition. Optional dance auditions are held late in the day, following the acting auditions.

National Dinner Theatre Association

National Dinner Theatre Association, P.O. Box 726, Marshall, MI 49068

Contact person: David M. Pritchard

Auditions take place around the second week of March. The location varies from year to year. In 1995, auditions were held in Indianapolis, Indiana. Approximately fifteen dinner theatres are represented at this audition. Auditionees must be eighteen at the time the application to audition is submitted. The deadline is about one week prior to the day of the audition. The audition fee is twenty-five dollars.

Audition Format: You are allowed one minute plus sixteen bars of music. Dance auditions are scheduled following the acting auditions.

New England Theatre Conference

New England Theatre Conference, Department of Theatre, Northeastern University, 360 Huntington Avenue, Boston, MA 02115

Contact person: Corey Boniface

Auditions are held in late March within the Boston area. Approximately sixty-five theatres are represented at these auditions. The application deadline is in early February. Auditions are open to non-Equity and Equity membership candidates only. Equity members are not eligible to apply. Companies offer summer and year-round employment. The audition fee is twenty-five dollars for NETC members, student nonmembers pay thirty-five dollars and nonstudent nonmembers pay forty dollars.

Audition Format: Performers are given a total of two minutes to present two brief, contrasting selections. Singers should prepare one song and one brief monologue or two musical numbers. Nonsingers should prepare two contrasting monologues. Singers and dancers must supply their own sheet music. An accompanist is provided and will not transpose any music. It is strongly recommended that no applicant sing or dance without an accompanist. Taped accompaniment is not advised.

NETC provides tips for those who audition. Suggestions are made about dress, selection of material, and making sure actors "get help from an experienced director or coach when preparing their selections." Actors are urged "to prepare their selections carefully within the established time limit of two minutes, in order to showcase their talent to the best advantage."[16] The complete list of audition tips is provided by the organization within their audition packet.

New Jersey Theatre Group

New Jersey Theatre Group, P.O. Box 21, Florham Park, NJ 07932
   Contact person: George Ryan
   Auditions are held in New Jersey twice each year, once in late August for two days and again in February for one day only. Equity-eligible and noneligible actors may audition. Notices that detail how to apply for an audition slot are in *Backstage* and other trade papers as well as at Actors' Equity and in the *Star-Ledger* six weeks prior to the audition. Approximately twenty Equity companies participate in this audition. Actors are chosen by a lottery. At each audition, there are approximately two hundred slots that the actors are auditioning for. There is no audition fee.

Audition Format: Each actor is allowed a total of two minutes to audition. The actor is free to do whatever he or she likes at the audition. If an actor chooses to sing, accompaniment is provided.

An actor may also sing a cappella. Taped accompaniment is not allowed.

Northwest Drama Conference

Northwest Drama Conference, Theatre Arts Department, University of Idaho, Moscow, ID 83843

Contact person: David Krasner

Auditions are held each year in February. The site of the audition changes each year. In 1995, it was held at the University of Oregon.

The application deadline for this audition is around the middle of January. The audition is open to anyone. Actors will need to contact NWDC regarding the fees to audition.

Audition Format: Each actor is allowed a total of four minutes. You may choose to do two monologues at two minutes each, or one song and one monologue. An accompanist is provided for the audition, but actors may sing a cappella or use taped accompaniment.

Ohio Theatre Alliance

Ohio Theatre Alliance, 77 South High Street, Second Floor, Columbus, OH 43215

Contact person: Eric Weisheit, Auditions Chair

Auditions are held around the second week of February. The location may vary, but in 1995 the event was held in Columbus, Ohio. Between forty and fifty producing companies and graduate schools are represented for summer and year-round positions. The auditions are held on two sites. At one site, actors audition for professional summer companies. At the second site, actors audition for graduate schools and professional companies looking for year-round performers. You must indicate on your audition form at which site(s) you want to audition. Actors are allowed to audition at both sites at no additional cost. The application deadline is in mid-January.

Those who audition must be a member of the Ohio Theatre Alliance. The director of your theatre must review your application and agree that you are qualified for the positions indicated on the application. The audition fee is twenty-five dollars for acting. If you are acting and doing a tech interview, the fee is thirty dollars. There is a five-dollar late fee added if the application is postmarked after the application deadline. OTA membership is thirty dollars for nonstudents and fifteen dollars for students.

Audition Format: All actors are given a total of two minutes to audition. The audition could include a monologue, or monologues, and a song, or songs. Singers must supply a battery-operated cassette recorder with prerecorded accompaniment. OTA furnishes no equipment.

Southeastern Theatre Conference

Southeastern Theatre Conference, Inc., P.O. Box 9868, Greensboro, NC 27429

Contact person: Marian A. Smith

The Southeastern Theatre Conference runs two auditions per year. The first is held during the first week of March. The annual spring auditions are held in a different city each year within the ten-state region. At this audition between 90 and 95 companies will see nearly 850 actors. Actors will be considered for summer and full-time positions. College actors who wish to participate in the Southeastern Theatre Conference auditions must go through a state screening process. Each state within the region has an allocation for the total number of auditionees they can send from the state. Also, for each state, a certain number of alternates are selected who will fill slots in case people selected decide they cannot go to the spring auditions for any reason. College actors from outside the region may participate in the state screening auditions by going to an audition at one of the border state auditions. Actors from out of the region should contact the SETC main office to discover which border state they are eligible to go to. These state screening auditions are held in October, November, or December.

Audition Format: SETC prints the following list of rules for auditionees:

1. Actors currently enrolled in a college or university, whether or not they have earned a salary acting, must attend the preliminary state auditions.
2. All state auditionees must be eighteen years or older, be enrolled in a college, or be a nonprofessional nonstudent at the time of application.
3. Preliminary auditionees will be accepted only in the state in which they are registered in school.

4. Preliminary auditionees outside the SETC region must apply to assigned SETC states for auditions. Contact your theatre department head or director for time and place of these auditions, fees to be charged, and application forms and instructions.
5. Professional actors and all persons attending only the dance auditions will apply directly to the SETC office for forms; preliminary auditions are not necessary. Professional actors are those who have worked in at least two professional productions since they have finished their training, received a salary, and have a director or producer who will recommend them by signing their acting audition application.
6. No actors will be allowed to change states for auditions screening.

Each state has its own audition fee structure so actors should contact their state organization for this information. Membership convention registration and audition fees due to SETC are as follows: student actors, total $40; adult nonprofessional actors, total $85.

Audition Procedures

1. All auditionees are required to fill out the entire audition application form by typewriter and to attach a current photo, sized to fit the space allowed on the form.
2. Auditions will be held on Thursday, Friday, and Saturday. The auditionee must audition on the day that corresponds to the audition number assigned.
3. Mandatory Audition Briefings will be held at 9:00 a.m. on Thursday, 10:00 a.m. on Friday, and 9:00 a.m. on Saturday. Your briefing is on the day of your audition.
4. The audition may consist of singing and acting, presented at the same time. All auditionees must tell the timekeeper if acting only, or acting and singing, or singing only before going on stage. If acting only, the time limit is one minute; if singing only, the time limit is one minute; if singing and acting, the time limit is a total of one and a half minutes. There will be an audition accompanist available. Music must be in the correct key; the pianist will not transpose. Taped accompaniment and a cappella singing are not permitted. Auditionees cannot accompany themselves on a musical instrument.
5. Performers will audition in groups of twenty-five. At the end of each group, the companies will identify those actors that they wish to see at call backs. The audition numbers of those called back will be posted on a bulletin board under the headings of the particular companies. The location and general time frame for call backs will also be posted. A specific call back time should be established beforehand by signing an appointment sheet posted at the call back location, always a room in the hotel where the auditions are held. Questions about this procedure will be addressed at the Mandatory Audition Briefing.
6. Dance auditions will be held for actors at the end of each day's audition. Details at Mandatory Briefing.

7. Dancers only will audition on Thursday afternoon, at approximately 4:00 p.m.
8. At the call back, the auditionee should be prepared to distribute her resume and head shot, to repeat the audition material, to present additional material, and to read from material provided by the company. Time is limited; while an auditionee may see ten or twelve companies, a company may see as many as seventy-five auditionees.
9. Some companies audition performers at locations other than SETC. For these organizations, final casting decisions may not be made until several weeks after the SETC auditions. Other companies may offer contracts on the spot. Most companies however, will collect resumes and pictures to keep on file. If a call back is received, it's a good idea for auditionees to drop the company a card during the coming months if their address on the resume changes.
10. Some openings listed by the various companies will be apprenticeships, rather than fully paid summer jobs. Check your roster of auditioning companies for this information. Theatre lists will be passed out on your audition day.
11. Fill out application form and preregistration form, attach money order and self-addressed stamped (#10 business size) envelope to forms; mail to State Coordinator, not to SETC.[17]

The Southeastern Theatre Conference also holds auditions in the fall for professional actors. These auditions are smaller than the spring auditions. Between thirty and thirty-five companies attend this audition looking to hire professional actors for full-time employment. This audition takes place in early September. The application deadline is in mid-August.

Anyone who auditions must be a member of SETC to audition. If the actor is already a member prior to the audition, the audition fee is ten dollars. For those who are not members prior to the audition must pay forty dollars to join SETC and the ten dollar audition fee for a total of fifty dollars.

For the fall auditions the format is the same as the spring auditions (see numbers four and five of the previous audition procedures).

Theatre Alliance of Michigan

Theatre Alliance of Michigan, P.O. Box 726, Marshall, MI 49068
 Contact person: David M. Pritchard, Auditions Coordinator
 Auditions take place around the last week of February. In 1995, this event was held at Western Michigan University in

Kalamazoo, but the location does change. In the past, around fifteen theatres have been represented at this audition.

The application deadline is a week prior to the audition. A late fee of five dollars is charged for all forms that arrive after the deadline. The audition fee is twenty-five dollars, which includes your membership into TAM.

Audition Format: Each actor who auditions is given two minutes to do two contrasting monologues plus sixteen bars of music. Dance auditions are scheduled in the afternoon of each day.

Southwest Theatre Association

Southwest Theatre Association, P.O. Box 10661, College Station, TX 77842

Contact person: Mickey D. Best, Audition Chair

The Southwest Theatre Association is made up of theatres in five states: Arkansas, Louisiana, New Mexico, Oklahoma, and Texas. It holds three auditions, one for high school seniors looking to get into a college program; one for college seniors looking for a graduate program; and one for professionals. The high school and graduate school auditions are held during the annual fall (November) conference. The professional auditions occur in January, or the Saturday of the Regions' American College Theatre Festival. The places of the auditions vary each year, so contact the organization regarding the place and times of the auditions.

All who audition must pay an audition fee (approximately fifteen dollars) and be a member of the Southwest Theatre Conference (forty dollars individual membership, fifteen dollars student membership).

Audition Format:

High School Auditions: Five minutes total are allowed for students to do a serious monologue and a comedic monologue followed by a song. No accompanist is provided. Students may bring a cassette tape. The tape recorder is provided.

Graduate School Auditions: The auditions are limited to three minutes. The students should present two contrasting pieces with the option of musical auditions using recorded music provided by the auditionee. Total time must not exceed three minutes. The students are asked simply to announce their selections and begin the audition with no introductions. They are also asked to bring head shots and resumes for distribution during call backs and interviews.

Professional Auditions: The acting auditions must not exceed one minute. The music portion is not to exceed sixteen bars. An accompanist is available. Actors may use their own cassette tape recorder or one provided by the organization if they prefer to use taped accompaniment.

Vermont Association of Theatres and Theatre Artists

Vermont Association of Theatres and Theatre Artists, 128 Elm Street, Montpelier, VT 05602

Contact person: Kim Bent or Wendi Stein

This audition takes place the second or third week of March. The audition is usually held at St. Michael's College, Winooski, but the site is renegotiated each year. Applications should be received by the first of March.

There are twelve to fifteen theatre companies with summer seasons in Vermont that attend this audition. About half of these companies are strictly non-Equity, and the others use some form of Equity contract, though most hire some non-Equity as well. In addition, casting people and representatives from film, commercial, and video production companies have been invited to attend these auditions.

First eligibility preference is given to Vermont residents and students at Vermont colleges. If space is still available, audition slots will then be allotted to residents of adjoining areas in New York, New Hampshire, and Massachusetts. Space will not be allotted to performers from the New York City or Boston areas, as they will be seen by the companies at auditions in those cities.

Performers' fees include a ten-dollar processing fee for VATTA, AEA, and GBTAE members; twenty-dollar audition fee for nonmembers. (VATTA's annual membership is ten dollars for students, twenty-five dollars for adults; GBTAE's membership is twelve dollars for individuals, fifty dollars for producers). Fees for designers and technical and management staff are ten dollars regardless of membership.

Audition Format: Performers will have three minutes in which to perform two contrasting monologues, plus sixteen or more bars of a song. The song is optional. At least one of the contrasting monologues should be contemporary. Singers should bring their own taped accompaniment; a cassette tape recorder will be provided. Performers will be assigned an audition time and should arrive at least one half hour prior to this time.

These are professional auditions, and applicants are expected to have considerable experience and/or preprofessional training. Applicants will be screened by a representative of VATTA to meet professional standards. Applicants who have not auditioned professionally before are advised to seek help from a teacher or director in preparing their resume and audition pieces.

So, You Want to 5
Go to Graduate
School?

*T*here are many good graduate programs around the country. Each department is different, so it is important really to shop around and gather information on the various programs to discover which one will give you the education you desire. Find several programs that seem to fit your needs best and make arrangements to visit each campus. Be sure to talk with faculty and with students who are in the program. After these visits you should be able to narrow down your search to at least three schools. Now, it is time to apply to these universities. Be careful not to put all your eggs in one basket and apply to only one school. Give yourself several options to see where you can get the best deal.

Admission requirements vary from school to school. Some will depend heavily on your overall grade point average (GPA), while others may look more at the grades within your major. Some will depend on your Graduate Record Exam (GRE) scores while others may not require them. However, all schools will require an audition and interview and will place heavy emphasis on how well you perform at both.

Again, each school is different, but from the interviews I have done with a number of major programs, there are some constants. This is what I will address in this chapter.   *59*

1. At the interview, show the directors that you are an intelligent and pleasant person who they will enjoy having in their program. In graduate school, faculty and students will spend many hours working one-on-one, and it is important that you work well together. Faculty are searching for mature, intelligent, and dependable individuals to serve as graduate assistants. Often these graduate students will be expected to teach a variety of undergraduate classes. Assistantships are highly competitive, so it is imperative that through your actions and dress at your interview, you convince the faculty that you are the best candidate for consideration. Let them know that you are someone they will want to work with for the next three years.

2. Often the interview time is not long enough for the directors to get a clear picture of who you are. Therefore, it becomes important that you use your audition pieces to say something about yourself. As Richard Nichols, a professor at Penn State told me, "The interview time is very tight so we really need to see the person in the audition piece. Students should not select pieces that mask who they are as a person."[18] As with all auditions, it is important for you to pick material that shows you at your best. It doesn't really matter what you choose to do as long as you do it well. The character should be your character type and someone you can play now. This will allow a sense of believability in your work. If you relate to the material and it touches your emotions, then your work will be honest and real. This will allow the directors to get a better picture of who you are as a person and as an actor.

3. Some directors will tell you not to do a piece in a dialect. As with other auditions, if you do not do dialects extremely well, avoid them. The dialect can work against you because it does not allow the director to see you; it will pull the director out of the piece, causing him or her to become overly aware of the dialect rather than listening to the character and believing what you are saying. The same can be said about doing period pieces. You must be comfortable with the piece and do it well or it will not be believable to the director. Don't choose a piece just because you feel you have to do it. Choose the piece because you relate to the character's personality and situation and you know you can make the words come to life. Jim Wren, an acting teacher at the University of North Carolina at Greensboro, gave me an excellent analogy that helps make this point clear. "If you are running a hundred-

yard dash in a track meet, why put high hurdles in your lane when the next person has a clear lane? Don't let stuff get in your way."[19] Jim is right; never allow any "stuff"—be it dialects, a fear of the classics, or whatever—to get in your way and keep you from doing well. These directors want to see your best work and nothing less. So choose an audition piece that will allow you to do your best. The result will be work that is honest, believable, and exciting and will allow the director to see different aspects of you.

4. Don't depend on props or costumes at this audition. Dress in nice clothing that really exhibits you in a pleasant light. If the piece requires props, it may not be the best piece to do. Often the way you use the props will draw the director's attention away from what you as the character want to say. You want the focus on you.

5. As with any audition, choose a piece that goes somewhere. As Jonathan Michaelsen at the University of Alabama told me, "Do something that is active; don't just tell us a story."[20] Your audition piece needs to show a character actively pursuing a strong objective. The piece must build to a climax and have a beginning, middle, and end.

6. Vocal work will weigh heavily at an audition. Regardless of the piece, you must show vocal variety, projection, enunciation, and energy. Regardless of the type of piece you do, through your use of voice and gesture you must, as George Crook at the University of Southern Mississippi says, "show an understanding of the language."[21] Much of this comes through preparation. Be well prepared so that you are at ease with your piece. Rehearse it aloud, taking time for pauses so you know the words are clear and the running time is well within the audition time frame. By being relaxed, you will look professional and you will make a good impression on the directors.

Finally, keep the audition in perspective. It is only an audition, not brain surgery. Do not put too much importance on any one audition. With every audition there is a chance you will not get the position you seek. If you do not, it does not mean you are a failure. Perhaps you were not the right character type. This can easily be the case at an MFA audition, especially if the program is tied into a professional company. If they already have plenty of ingenues and you are an ingenue, then they may not need you and you will not be cast. You never know what a director is looking for. Do not try to second guess the director. Go out and focus on your character and the character's objectives. Make sure you give the best audition possible. If you are not hired, then it's not anyone's fault. Do not dwell on what happens. Learn from the experience and go on to other auditions. If you continue to work hard and give your best, some university or company will use you. Remember, auditions are not personal; they are business. Many factors go into a director's decision and most of these are factors over which you have no control. Just do your best and be prepared to accept the consequences whatever they might be.

U/RTA: University/Resident Theatre Association

The largest consortium of professional training programs in the United States is the University/Resident Theatre Association or U/RTA. Each year they offer several hundred positions. Through engagements with graduate programs, participation in Shakespeare festivals, involvement in resident theatre companies on and off college campuses and other related activities, U/RTA gives out over $1.5 million dollars in first-year allowances. Member institutions include: University of Alabama/Alabama Shakespeare Festival, University of Arizona/Arizona Repertory Theatre, University of California–Irvine, University of Connecticut /Connecticut Repertory Theatre, Florida State University/ASOLO, University of Florida, University of Georgia/Georgia Repertory Theatre, Illinois State University/Illinois Shakespeare Festival, University of Illinois–Urbana–Champaign, Indiana University, University of Iowa/Iowa Summer Rep, Michigan State University, University of Minnesota/the Guthrie Theatre, University of Missouri–Kansas City/Missouri Repertory Theatre, University of Nebraska–Lincoln/Nebraska Repertory Theatre, Northern Illinois University/SummerNITE, Northwestern University, Ohio State University, Pennsylvania State University/Pennsylvania Centre Stage, University of Pittsburgh/Three Rivers Shakespeare, Purdue University/Purdue Summer Theatre, Rutgers University, University of South Carolina/the Shakespeare Theatre, University of Southern California, Southern Methodist University, Temple University, University of Texas–Austin, Utah Shakespearean Festival, University of Washington, Wayne State University, West Virginia University, and the University of Wisconsin–Madison.

All acting candidates are required to attend a screening audition. These screening auditions are held in three locations, New York, New York (late January or early February), Evanston, Illinois (mid-February), and Irvine, California (early March). Candidates are evaluated here by qualified adjudicators who will supply each candidate with a written response that includes comments, recommendations, and, if appropriate, instructions on improving the presentations for the final audition, which is held the next day. No contracts are offered by prospective school programs, festivals, or theatres at the screening audition. Usually you audition during the day; then that evening you are called back to discover if you have been passed on to the finals.

If passed to the final auditions, the following day you will perform your audition pieces for representatives from the U/RTA schools and theatres along with special guest members from other universities and regional theatres. Following the final presentations these representatives will interview those candidates in whom they are interested.

Firm offers are not made to any candidates prior to the end of the first week of March. The fee for this audition is sixty-five dollars. Any recipient or imminent recipient of an undergraduate degree is eligible to attend this audition. The application deadline is around the end of November.

Audition Format: Participants in the U/RTA acting auditions should adhere to the following U/RTA guidelines. It is also recommended that you follow the guidelines in the *Handbook for Actors and Coaches*, which is supplied by U/RTA upon receipt of your complete application.

1. Secure an audition coach, preferably one familiar with U/RTA auditions, who will help you prepare your audition.
2. Select two contrasting pieces, one of which may be classical and/or verse.
3. Choose material well within your present maturity and casting range.
4. Props, costumes, and elaborate staging are discouraged.
5. Avoid overused selections.
6. Limit your introduction to play title and character's name. A U/RTA host will introduce you by name to the auditors.
7. Introductions, monologues, and transitions may not exceed a total of four minutes.
8. Sixteen bars of a song, not to exceed thirty seconds, may be sung in addition to the two monologues. Provide your own accompaniment on a prerecorded cassette tape. A cappella singing is not acceptable. The sixteen bars are not included in your four-minute time limit. A cassette player will be provided

for you at the audition site.

9. If you are interested in Shakespeare festivals and have not included a classical piece in your audition package, please have one prepared at the call backs.

10. Be sure to bring one copy of your head shot and resume with you to the screening auditions and be prepared to bring at least ten copies to the final auditions should you be passed on.[22]

The Handbook for Actors and Coaches was prepared by Robert E. Leonard at Penn State University. It gives the applicant tips on selection of material, preparing and presenting the audition, and other pertinent information. It is an excellent guide for actors to use in preparing for this audition.

As stated earlier, U/RTA will supply you with a copy of this handbook upon receipt of your completed application. For more information you may write to Gina G. Cesari, University/Resident Theatre Association, Inc., 1560 Broadway, Suite 903, New York, NY 10036, or call (212) 221-1130.

The Irene Ryan Acting Scholarship

Background

The Irene Ryan Acting Scholarship was established in 1971. Ms. Ryan, who is probably best remembered for her role of "Granny" on the television show *The Beverly Hillbillies,* set up this scholarship to assist struggling young actors who wanted to get into the business. Kingsley Colton, executive director of the Irene Ryan Foundation, explained, "She attended the auditions during their first year in 1972. Later, Ms. Ryan collapsed on stage while performing in the Broadway production of *Pippin,* and two days prior to the presentation of the 1973 Irene Ryan Acting Scholarship auditions she passed away. She left her entire fortune to the Irene Ryan Foundation, which over the years has helped to finance the training of many talented young actors."[23]

Each year the Irene Ryan Foundation awards scholarships and fellowships. Sixteen of these are regional awards consisting of a $500 scholarship for each regional winner. There are also two national awards of $2,500 each for the winners of the competition, which is held during the national American College Theatre Festival at the Kennedy Center in Washington, D.C. One national finalist receives a scholarship from the Society of American Fight Directors to attend their National Stage Combat Workshop. In addition, a student is chosen to be "best partner" at the national festival and is awarded a $500 scholarship. The Irene Ryan Foundation sends the scholarship money to a school designated by each winner, where it is to be used to pay tuition and fees for further education, not necessarily limited to theatre.

Guidelines

Guidelines for the Irene Ryan Acting Scholarships are printed for those entered in the American College Theatre Festival. The following is a list of the guidelines supplied by the American College Theatre Festival. These guidelines apply to Irene Ryan competitions at both regional and national levels.

1. Only those performers who have appeared in either a participating or associate American College Theatre Festival entry and are bona fide students in a college or university at the time of the American College Theatre Festival official adjudication are eligible. Eligible students must be: an undergraduate student registered for at least six semester or equivalent quarter hours; or a graduate student registered for at least three semester or equivalent quarter hours; or a continuing part-time student enrolled in a regular degree or certificate program. All undergraduate, graduate, and continuing part-time students who participate must be enrolled in a college or university working toward a degree.
2. The chair of the theatre department (or the equivalent academic officer) must verify the student's and partner's status in writing to the regional chair prior to the Regional Festival's Irene Ryan Competition.
3. The director of a participating or associate production is responsible for informing all eligible students of the Irene Ryan rules.
4. Each college or university may nominate one student performer from the cast of each of its participating or associate entries. A maximum of two nominations from each participating and associate entry may be made by American College Theatre Festival representatives.
5. The regional chair or delegate shall notify each of the nominees of his or her selection as an Irene Ryan competitor.
6. Each competitor shall bear all expenses of attending the regional festival (unless these expenses are otherwise provided for within the region). Transportation, lodging, and a per diem allowance are provided for each national festival competitor and for each partner, only if the actor can be present for the National Festival's Saturday evening rehearsal at the Kennedy Center. If a regional finalist cannot be present for the National Festival's Saturday evening rehearsal at the Kennedy Center, the additional airfare for his/her Sunday

arrival will not be the responsibility of the Kennedy Center or the American College Theatre Festival. The Saturday evening Irene Ryan rehearsal at the Kennedy Center is a closed rehearsal. Only candidates, their partners, and accompanists are allowed to attend. Coaches of students may attend the Sunday dress rehearsal but will not be admitted to the Saturday night rehearsal.

7. Not more than sixteen nominees shall appear in final competition at the regional festival. In those regions where more than sixteen competitors qualify for the regional festival, a screening system will be determined by the regional chair. The screening system should insure that no nominee should perform more than twice on any day, so screening and final rounds may be scheduled over a two-day period. Whenever possible, prescreening rounds should be combined with an audition workshop.

8. The regional prescreening and final competition normally will occur prior to any of the productions scheduled to perform at the regional festival. However, when the regional chair can use final-round judges who have not seen festival productions prior to the final round, that round may be held any time.

9. The final round of the regional festival must not be judged by academic professionals affiliated with regional institutions.

10. The names of the winner and the first alternate shall be communicated first to the regional chair and subsequently announced at a time designated by the chair.

11. Material for Irene Ryan auditions must be selected from one of three sources: 1) material in the public domain; 2) material written for or by the candidate; and 3) material for which the actor can obtain in writing the rights for performance. If the nominee obtains permission to use published material no cuts or changes can be made in that material. Written proof of permission from the rights holder must be presented at each level of the Irene Ryan competition.

    The American College Theatre Festival will pay any royalties for material presented in the National "Evening of Scenes" at the Kennedy Center. A form for requesting performance rights from the copyright holder will be supplied to each actor when notified of his or her selection as an Irene Ryan competitor.

    Irene Ryan candidates selected to perform at the Kennedy Center's National Irene Ryan Evening of Scenes must provide his/her regional chair with proof of royalty clearance for the selected audition material within ten days of the close of the regional festival. All rights documentation will then be forwarded to the ACTF national office. If the candidate is unable to provide rights clearance documentation, the regional chair reserves the right to send the Irene Ryan regional alternate to the National American College Theatre Festival at the Kennedy Center.

12. Each candidate and partner shall be introduced by name and selection only.

13. A rehearsal shall be scheduled in the performance space before the final round of competition.
14. Only basic lighting is permitted and will be provided by the host theatre for the rehearsal and performance.
15. When a performer has been qualified for competition at the regional festival, he should carefully choose two contrasting scenes to be presented at the festival. The presentation shall be limited to five minutes, including transitions between scenes. Timing of the audition will begin with the first action or word in character following the set-up and introduction. Participants exceeding the five-minute time limit risk disqualification. Audition pieces will be timed at every level of competition, including the Irene Ryan Evening of Scenes at the Kennedy Center. Any performer exceeding the five-minute limit at the Kennedy Center National Festival performance will be disqualified.
16. The Irene Ryan audition must be composed of two separate selections. At least one selection must be a scene performed with a partner who is a bona fide student at the time of initial screening. Irene Ryan competitors may not perform with other Irene Ryan competitors. If both selections are performed with another actor, the same person must be used in both instances. If a musical number is one of the two scenes, the accompanist will not count as the partner. At the regional level, an Irene Ryan partner may serve as a partner a maximum of two times per festival.
17. It is recommended that no costume as such be used. A costume accessory may be used.
18. It is recommended that no more than two or three pieces of furniture, such as a chair, stool, or table, be used. These basic set pieces will be provided by the host. If simple hand props are used, they must be provided by the competitor.
19. Each regional finalist in the Irene Ryan competition must provide the regional chair with two black-and-white, eight-by-ten photos labeled with his/her name, permanent address, and school address. The Irene Ryan candidate selected as the regional finalist must provide to his or her regional chair (within one week of the closing of the regional festival) the name of the school and the administrative official at that school to whom the regional scholarship funds should be directed. The regional chair will forward this information to Kingsley Colton, executive director of the Irene Ryan Foundation.[24]

Choosing Your Material

I have spoken with a variety of directors from around the country about the Irene Ryan Acting Scholarship auditions to discover what really makes a good audition package. I don't believe there is any one particular formula for success, but I can make a few helpful suggestions.

Find your pieces early and make sure you can get permission from the publisher to perform them at the festival. There is no reason to work on material that you will not be allowed to perform. Pick the material early and immediately submit your request for permission to use the piece.

As you search for material, try to find pieces that you understand and can easily relate to. At the same time, make sure that the material is universal enough to appeal to an audience regardless of their backgrounds. Troy State University's David Dye said, "The actor's piece must touch us in some way."[25] The characters you choose should be your age and character type. As with other auditions, choose material that you could be cast in now and be sure the piece is within your vocal and physical range. You will be doing two pieces so make sure they contrast. The adjudicators will want to see three completely different characters at this audition: first, you as the narrator, second, you as character number one, and third, you as character number two. You should work in rehearsals to make all three characters clear to your audience. Strong contrasting pieces, along with specific physical and vocal choices, will allow you to do this.

Pieces should be active; that is to say, they must go somewhere. Make sure your character has powerful obstacles to overcome and that you are working to overcome these obstacles throughout the piece. The character needs to be in some type of crisis. As you work on your objectives to resolve the crises at hand, the piece will be active.

As with all audition pieces try to find material from sources that are not "hot" properties. Look for plays that are in the public domain. Search for material from sources other than plays. Again, novels, short stories, journals, and essays can all be appropriate sources. Deborah Anderson, regional chair of Region IV of ACTF said, "It is important to find unique material."[26] Such material will keep you from being compared to others and will help you find pieces that will require no letters of permission or payment of royalty fees.

Make sure the pieces you do for the Irene Ryan Acting Scholarship auditions do not require a dialect. Dialects at this audition will get in your way, for some adjudicators will become aware of the dialect and stop listening to the character. This will pull them out of the scene and as a result you will not make the finals. Do pieces in standard American stage dialect.

Working the Piece

Once the material is chosen, you must pick your partners. At least one of the pieces you do must be a two-character scene. The choice of the right partner is extremely important. As David Dye said,"Choose a partner who is equally proficient in the development of the scene."[27] I have seen young actors pick their best friend, or a lover, for a partner because they like them. They do not take into consideration the talent of the individual or whether or not the person chosen is right for the scene. Find the strongest actor possible who fits the other character in your scene and who will work with you as a team player. Remember, you are the one nominated for the scholarship. The scene must showcase your abilities. At the same time, the adjudicators will want to see two actors talking to one another, listening to each other, and truly finding a communion on stage.

As you begin rehearsals, remember that you are putting together a total package. No part of this five-minute audition can be weak. The mistake I often see actors make is that they work on their scene and monologue without thinking about the introduction, conclusion, or transitions in and out of scenes. Do not wait until the end of the rehearsal process to put the entire package together. Work on all parts of the audition, placing furniture, introductions, entrances, and exits as well as the acting of the pieces. To make the finals of the Irene Ryan auditions, your work must be more polished than any other audition you will ever do.

The following are separate components that must be polished during the rehearsal process:

1. You enter the space. As with all auditions, your audition begins when they see you. Be pleasant, courteous, and professional.
2. You set your furniture. Move pieces of furniture with a purpose. Do not drag furniture. Once the set is in place, do not move or adjust it again. Moving furniture should be done at a quick, but not hectic, pace.
3. As soon as your furniture is set, move directly to your starting position. Come to a full stop; when ready, take a deep breath

and begin your introduction. Will York of Auburn University advises, "The introduction must show insight into the personality of the individual."[28] Let them see the real you with your introduction. Be open with the audience, talking to them and not at them. Also, make sure the introduction is as concise as possible. You want to give the adjudicators your names and the names of the pieces and authors. Nothing more is needed.

4. Your time will begin with your first word or movement following the introduction. Take a moment and breathe deeply. This will allow you time for a transition from you, the actor, into you, the first character.

5. Whenever you finish the first piece, use a change of body posture and a very brief pause to make the transition into the second character. You, your coach, and your partner will need to decide which scene or monologue you should do first. It really doesn't matter, as long as the transitions in and out of the pieces are clean and slick.

6. Another transition will be needed out of the second character into the conclusion. Hold your final moment in a short tableau for a brief period of time. Let us see you come out of this with another physical transition from the second character back into the actor. Face the audience, stand still, smile, take a deep breath, give your names again, say "thank you" and then start your exit.

7. As you exit, leave the stage as if you gave an Oscar-winning performance. No matter how you feel inside about the piece, always exit in a state of elation. If you set furniture at the top of the scene, be sure to block into your exit an organized and swift strike of all furniture and props.

At the Audition

As with all auditions, dress is very important. David Dye said it best when he said, "Dress to enhance the mood of the piece and the character you are portraying."[29] Your clothes should be easy to move in, should help to complement your body, and should, in a theatrical way, express the character you are playing. This does not mean you need to wear a costume; just dress to make yourself look good and to enhance the pieces you are doing.

Throughout the audition, make certain you show assurance in your abilities. It does not pay to be cocky, but you must look cool and confident. This will show through your use of voice and body language. Be aware of these things and make sure you are sending the right message to anyone who sees you at the audition (on or off the stage).

Your audition lasts a total of five minutes. Make sure in your rehearsals that your time is far less than this. As you saw in the guidelines, you can be disqualified for going over the time limit. Deborah Anderson even suggests that the audition be around "four minutes in length."[30] This will allow you plenty of time for transitions. If, subconsciously, you know you have lots of time, you will not rush anything, allowing you to discover correct rhythms and tempos and making for a much stronger audition.

Another area you must take into consideration as you go into performance is the space. This is particularly true at the regional level where the space you perform in may range from a classroom to a small studio theatre to a large auditorium. Be prepared to perform your piece in any space. Rehearse it in all sizes of spaces so you can easily adapt what you do. Make your voice and body movements conform to any space you are given.

Summary

When asked what is important at this audition, Will York stressed three things:

1. "The ability to act well,"
2. "Appropriate and interesting material that shows range," and
3. "The personality of the individual."[31]

All three of these will play a part at this audition. You must put together a strong, polished package if you hope to make the finals. Something in your personality, your choice of piece, and your acting ability must be unequaled, causing you to stand out and become a finalist out of hundreds of auditionees. Be prepared and endeavor to do your best. Don't worry about the outcomes of the audition. Always remember, being nominated for an Irene Ryan Acting Scholarship is in itself an honor.

Auditioning for a Local Commercial or Industrial Film

7

Getting Started

Many young actors are unaware of the possibilities of getting work as "talent" in local commercials and industrial films. I know many actors residing outside of New York City and Los Angeles who make a decent living in this way.

To get started, look in your phone book and find out if there are any casting agents, talent agencies, or modeling agencies listed. Contact them by sending a letter of introduction, a resume, and head shot. You will find in this medium, the head shot becomes even more important than it is for live theatre. The picture will be your business card, so make sure you have plenty of professional-looking glossy, black-and-white, eight-by-ten head shots.

Following the letter, call the agency or casting agent and find out if they are interested in you. In this business, you must be persistent but not pushy. Try to arrange an interview with them, so they have a chance to see you in person and you can charm them with your personality.

Some modeling agencies will want you to pay huge fees to them for classes, pictures, and so forth. Before paying anything, ask for references and determine if they are a legitimate business that has helped other actors in your area find work. The actor's grapevine is usually the best source to discover if you will benefit by signing with a specific agency.

Over the years, I have done well without an agency representing me. In a small market this is possible, but in larger cities the agency will be important in helping you get work. You usually will get the agent by either being referred from another source (director, producer, and other actors) or by knocking on doors.

With television, the eyes become extremely important. Television is a close-up medium. Therefore, with your photos and at auditions, make sure you do everything you can to make your eyes stand out. In this medium, stay away from clothes that are solid white, solid black, or that have horizontal stripes. Also avoid bright or shiny clothing and shirts that have any writing on them. At these auditions wear more muted colors. Blue is an especially strong color to wear. Plaids also seem to look good on camera.

The Audition

Always go to an audition very early. It will help you to arrive at least thirty minutes prior to your call. As with all auditions be very polite to anyone you meet. Look everyone in the eye, smile, and shake their hand. You want to make a good impression on the receptionist, the crew, the director, and anyone else involved.

When you first arrive, be sure to sign in. Now, try to find out everything you can about the audition. Ask if you can see the storyboard and a script. The storyboard looks much like a comic strip. It is used to set up each shot. In it you will see the blocking they plan to use, the props, costumes, and the type of shots (long, medium, and close-up). By seeing this, you can get a very good idea as to how to dress and how to block your audition. The office may not always supply a storyboard, but it never hurts to ask.

I have discovered that in television, casting directors and clients are often not willing to change preconceived ideas. They have already decided exactly what they want the commercial or industrial film to look like. They usually will not be willing to deviate from this concept. No matter how good you are at the audition, you will not persuade them to change their minds and cast you if you look different from their preconceived ideas. For this reason, get to the audition early. Talk with the receptionist, look at the storyboard, and try to find out all you can about what they want. Then transform yourself as best you can to look and sound like the character they are searching for. With television, dressing like the character is to your advantage. Always come to an audition dressed the way you think the character would dress. Also bring other choices with you. For example, suppose you hear they are casting a male detective and a housewife. As the male detective, you might show up in a suit and trench coat, trying to look like a "Bogart" or "Columbo" type of detective. You arrive at the audition to discover they want more of a "Baretta" or "Martin Riggs" (*Lethal Weapon*) type of character. In your car you have a sweatshirt, jeans, ball cap, and tennis shoes. Since you are there early, you now can go and change to look more like the character in the storyboard. For a woman trying to audition for the housewife, she may arrive in a very nice dress only to discover that the housewife in the commercial is wearing a sweat suit and tennis shoes. If she has arrived early enough, now is her time to change. Always take the opposite of what you think the character should wear to an audition. The more you look and act like the character in the storyboard, the better your chances to get cast. Whatever you wear to this audition, unless directed to do otherwise, wear the same thing to the call back. This will help them to remember you. Remember, if they give you a call back, then they liked you at the audition.

At this type of audition, get into character from the moment you walk into the door. They will often ask for your name and number before you begin. Do it in character. Remember, they are looking for a specific character type, so give it to them. I recently landed a commercial for a local bank. The character they wanted was a "redneck factory worker." I went to the audition dressed to fit the part and acting that way too. I got the part, and after the shoot was complete several days later, the director came up to me, shook my hand, and said that he enjoyed working with me. Then he gave me what I felt was a great compliment. He said, "When you auditioned we thought you were the real thing and even now we are not sure if you are or not." Then, for the first time, I came out of character and thanked him.

At the audition, you will probably get a short interview. You want to impress everyone there. The people who may be there will include the following: 1. The client (it is his or her product and money; he or she has a great influence on casting); 2. The casting director (his or her job is on the line; he or she will work hard to make you look good); 3. The agency (they wrote the commercial, so they have influence on casting); 4. The director (you must make a good impression on this person, as he or she makes the final decision); 5. The crew (they have little to say about whether or not you get hired, but be nice to them; they can make you look great or awful).

At some auditions you may be asked to give the director your name, number, and some information about yourself, while you show them a full front shot, a profile shot, and a back shot. This is called a slate. Do not be bland while doing this. Be sure to really bring your personality out when giving this information. At other auditions, you may get the chance to read a script with someone else. This is referred to as a combination. The following tips can be helpful when reading with someone:

1. Work to make as much eye contact as possible with your partner. Try to look into his or her downstage eye with your upstage eye. This sounds funny, but try it on a close-up shot on your own video camera. Your face will be more open and since the audience sees your eyes, you are making a stronger impression.

2. Get very close to your partner. This is not the stage. They don't want large movements and big gestures. The closer you get to your partner the better the shot.

3. Make sure you stay open to the camera. Do not acknowledge it unless you are told to do so, but keep your face and body open to it always.

4. Your reactions are extremely important. Reactions need to be honest and real. Don't act! Really listen and look at your partner. As stated earlier, do not have your face in your script. Talk to your partner, not at her; focus on her, not your audience.

5. If the script is stapled together you may want to take the staple out. This will allow you to read the script and casually drop discarded pages on the floor as you finish with them. Turning pages can draw attention away from the scene. To drop them off to the side will not draw as much attention especially if it is a tight shot. When finished, be sure to pick up the pages you have dropped and put the script back together again.

6. Keep your voice at a level that you would naturally have in a conversation in real life. Remember, you will wear a microphone and you do not need to project as you would on stage. The voice is clearly articulated and supported but it is not overdone. Never give the impression that you are "acting." You must look natural. The old adage of theatre, "less is more," really holds true on film.

7. Always remember that it is the product that is most important. Whatever you do in a scene, make the product stand out.
8. When you are finished, say "thank you," and then leave. These people are busy; do not waste their time with chit-chat. Be polite and leave.

A dear friend of mine, Marie Prater, is a casting director out of Birmingham. I have had the honor of working with her on several occasions and have had her teach some workshops to my students at UAB. She supplies her students with some excellent audition tips. The following is her list of things to consider at an audition.

Prater's Do's and Don't's

1. Don't walk in chattering.
2. Size up space without asking where to go.
3. Ask questions about script, character, and accent.
4. Ask for a prototype only if you can't devise one.
5. Listen to directions and adapt.
6. Listen to voice fluctuations when being directed.
7. Take a second to compose yourself.
8. Don't make excuses for bloops.
9. Never show facial expressions when you screw up.
10. Be conscious of your body language.
11. If there's activity behind the camera, don't acknowledge it.
12. Don't come with food or drink, nor should you smoke during an interview or audition.
13. Don't wear shiny, blousey, or gathered pants, or horizontal stripes.
14. Don't chew gum, unless it adds to the character.
15. Be aggressive to a point.[32]

Check List

Marie also supplies her students with the following "check list" to go through prior to a performance or audition.

1. Am I walking or running into the camera view, and what will be the first part of me to be seen? If your action is not seen by the camera it never happens to the viewer.
2. Where is the label on the product if I am to hold it? Can the viewer see the entire logo if I demonstrate the product? Where am I holding the product? Unless otherwise told, the product held by your face should be no lower than the bottom of the chest and no higher than your cheekbone. The product is then seen in an important place.

3. Do I drink from anything? You must cheat to the camera with a slight profile so that your facial expressions and reactions will be seen.
4. Do I understand the atmosphere that the scene is creating with the product? What is the tempo or rhythm that they want to create?
5. Always ask for a storyboard. If there is a scene-by-scene of the commercial, you will be able to understand what the director wants that actor to look like, be dressed like, to see the video and camera directions, etc.
6. Ultimately, you must build characters that are believable and have interesting relationships that help sell the product or service and that will focus on the benefits for the viewer. Don't worry about the business of the camera, lighting, or sound. The technicalities should never limit the creative flow of the performer.[33]

Industrial Films

Another area actors need to be aware of is work in industrial films. Industrial films are used by companies to train their employees or to give instruction to their customers. Actors are hired to play roles of company employees, clients, and so forth. These scripts are usually written and produced by the company itself. I have done several of these films, playing everything from a carpenter in a film on meter installation, to a marketing nerd in a film on marketing do's and don't's, to a foreman in a film on ball-crane safety. Power companies, gas companies, phone companies, libraries, and even the United States military make these films. Just about any large corporation has a department that is in charge of these projects. Call the companies, find out who is responsible for their training films, and be sure to contact them. Send them your photo and resume and try to get an interview. These people are always looking for new faces for their projects. In fact, after doing a few of these industrial films for a company, they will probably stop using you because they don't want their employees seeing the same actor in a variety of roles. Follow all of the rules that apply to commercial auditioning and you should do well.

Conclusion

Nothing an actor can do will insure that he or she will get a role at an audition. There are too many factors that will affect the outcome of the audition. Far too often just giving a good audition is not enough. The director may not want your type or perhaps your type has already been cast. Perhaps your hair or eyes are the wrong color or the director wanted someone two inches shorter than you. Perhaps on your resume you did not indicate that you could ride a bike and they really wanted someone who is an excellent bike rider. Or, the director cast a family member in your role who is not quite as good as you but it will make peace in the family to do so.

All you can do is be well prepared and give the best audition possible. If you get cast, excellent. If you do not get cast, don't worry about it. There will be other auditions. Never take rejection as if it reflects on your abilities as an actor. Be honest with yourself, and if you are absolutely sure you did the best job possible at the audition and you were not cast, then don't fret over it. It is not your fault! Nor is it the end of the world.

Do go to as many auditions as possible. The more you do, the more comfortable you will become with the process and the better your skills will become. Learn not only by doing but by observing. Much can be learned by watching both good and bad actors at an audition. Apply the techniques you learn and your audition skills will improve.

It will also help you to remember the casting directors you meet at auditions. Whether or not you get a role, be sure to send them a thank you note for giving you the chance to audition for them. Remember, nice guys will eventually be rewarded for their efforts. The directors may not use you this time, but if they remember you and like you, your chances of getting cast later are improved.

I hope you have found the techniques presented in this book to be helpful. I truly believe that if you use them, work will come your way. Never give up. Break a leg!

Notes

1. D. Ward Haarbauer, interview with the author, Birmingham, AL, April 1995.

2. Haarbauer, interview.

3. Sonia Moore, *The Stanislavski System: The Professional Training of an Actor* (Penguin, 1978), 4.

4. William Hardy, interview with the author, Norfolk, VA, March 1995.

5. David Weiss, interview with the author, Norfolk, VA, March 1995.

6. Weiss, interview.

7. Molly Risso, interview with the author, Norfolk, VA, March 1995.

8. Robert David Funk, *Women and the War: 1861–1865*, (Unpublished play, University of Alabama at Birmingham, 1992), 22–23.

9. ———, *Co. Aytch: Memoirs of a Confederate Soldier*, (Unpublished play, University of Alabama at Birmingham, 1986), 10–11.

10. ———, *Women and the War*, 20–21.

11. Shakespeare, *As You Like It*, act 3, scene 5, lines 43–53.

12. Moore, 40–41.

13. Uta Hagen, *Respect for Acting*, (Macmillan, 1973), 31.

14. Indiana Theatre Conference, "Indiana Theatre Conference Audition Tips" (Information provided in the organization's registration packet, Indianapolis, IN, 1995).

15. The Institute of Outdoor Drama, "Guidelines For Singers" (Information provided in the organization's confirmation packet, Chapel Hill, NC, 1995).

16. New England Theatre Conference, "The New England Theatre Conference 1994 Auditions Packet" (Audition tips are provided in the organization's audition packet, Boston, MA, 1994).

17. Southeastern Theatre Conference, "SETC Audition Application Form and Information for Student Actors and Adult Nonprofessional Actors" (Rules and procedures are printed in the SETC audition application form and information for student actors and adult nonprofessional actors, Greensboro, NC, 1994).

18. Richard Nichols, telephone interview with the author, May 1995.

19. Jim Wren, telephone interview with the author, May 1995.

20. Jonathan Michaelsen, telephone interview with the author, May 1995.

21. George Crook, telephone interview with the author, May 1995.

22. The University/Resident Theatre Association, "U/RTA Guidelines for the Application 1995 U/RTA National Unified Auditions and Interviews" (Information provided with U/RTA application guidelines, New York, NY, 1995).

23. Kingsley Colton, telephone interview with the author, May 1995.

24. The Kennedy Center American College Theatre Festival, "Guidelines for Irene Ryan Acting Award Scholarships Kennedy Center American College Theatre Festival" (Information provided in the Guidelines for Irene Ryan Acting Award Scholarships, Washington, DC, 1994).

25. David Dye, telephone interview with the author, April 1995.

26. Deborah Anderson, telephone interview with the author, May 1995.

27. Dye, interview.

28. Will York, telephone interview with the author, May 1995.

29. Dye, interview.

30. Anderson, interview.

31. York, interview.

32. Marie Prater, "Do's and Don't's" (Unpublished guide for actors, Birmingham, AL, 1994).

33. Marie Prater, "Audition Check List" (Unpublished guide for actors, Birmingham, AL, 1994).

Bibliography

Adler, Stella. *The Technique of Acting*. New York: Bantam Books. 1988.

Boleslavsky, Richard. *Acting: The First Six Lessons*. New York: Theater Arts Books, 1984.

Funk, Robert David. *Co. Aytch: Memoirs of a Confederate Soldier*. Unpublished play, Birmingham, 1986. Based on Watkins, Samuel R. *Co. Aytch: A Side Show of the Big Show*. Nashville: Cumberland Presbyterian, 1882.

———. *Women and the War: 1861–1865*. Unpublished play, Birmingham, 1992a. Based on Pember, Phoebe Yates. *A Southern Woman's Story: Life in Confederate Richmond*. New York: G.W. Carleton, 1879.

———. *Women and the War: 1861–1865*. Unpublished play, Birmingham, 1992b. Based on Beers, Fannie A. *Memories: A Record of Personal Experiences and Adventure During Four Years of War*. Lippincott, 1888.

Gordon, Mel. *The Stanislavsky Technique: Russia*. New York: Applause Theatre Book Publishers, 1988.

Hagen, Uta. *Respect For Acting*. New York: Macmillan, 1973.

Indiana Theatre Conference. "Indiana Theatre Conference Audition Tips." Indianapolis, 1995.

Institute of Outdoor Drama. "Guidelines For Singers." Chapel Hill, 1995.

The Kennedy Center American College Theatre Festival. "Guidelines for Irene Ryan Acting Award Scholarships

Kennedy Center American College Theatre Festival." Washington, 1994.

Moore, Sonia. *The Stanislavski System: The Professional Training of an Actor*. New York: Penguin, 1978.

New England Theatre Conference. "The New England Theatre Conference 1994 Auditions Packet." Boston, 1994.

Prater, Marie. "Audition Check List." Unpublished guide for actors, Birmingham, 1994.

———. "Do's and Don't's." Unpublished guide for actors, Birmingham, 1994.

Shakespeare, William. *As You Like It*. New York: Pocket Books, 1959.

Southeastern Theatre Conference. "SETC Audition Application Form and Information for Student Actors and Adult Nonprofessional Actors." Greensboro, 1994.

Stanislavski, Constantin. *An Actor Prepares*. New York: Theatre Art Books, 1984.

———. *Building a Character*. New York: Theatre Art Books, 1979.

———. *Creating a Role*. New York: Theatre Art Books, 1978.

The University/Resident Theatre Association. "U/RTA Guidelines for the Application, 1995 U/RTA National Unified Auditions and Interviews." New York, 1995.